WORKING in TIME

WORKING in TIME

KIEROY TAN

PARTRIDGE

A Penguin Random House Company

ISBN: Softcover   978-1-4828-3118-4
             eBook   978-1-4828-3119-1

Print information available on the last page.

To order additional copies of this book, contact
Toll Free 800 101 2657 (Singapore)
Toll Free 1 800 81 7340 (Malaysia)
orders.singapore@partridgepublishing.com

www.partridgepublishing.com/singapore

CONTENTS

INTRODUCTION

This book unearths the unwritten truths about work coming from a perspective of a young man growing up in a first world environment. In this era, many people have lost the drive and will to work for things or even earn it; many treat things as though it comes easily and freely, therefore do not know how to cherish the things of life and the simplicity of it. Humans believe that simple things are weak, but it is through simple things that people find joy in it. I write this to share my perspective with you; coming from a workaholic myself I hope that it could also help you. I write this with different perspective towards different things. If you feel that the hardest part is to start working, then this book is probably for you. It also tells you as a reader how I came up with such a perspective of things. Above all I hope it could give you a newer perspective on the up and coming generations. It starts with my personal point of view and experiences, opinions and ends with the idea of "what I have now I'll give it to you".

IMPORTANCE AND
GAIN OF WORK

In the beginning of time, man was created to work, and work was created for man. Work was created so that man could eat, drink, and find joy in it, and, more importantly, not know the future, therefore keeping man sane. Man had all the pleasures in life; good food, health, and all that man could ever ask for; even animals were subjected to and named by man. All man needed to do was to maintain the work given to him, with no additional stress or pressure. Work as defined by Oxford Dictionary, is an activity involving mental or physical effort done in order to achieve a result.

Without work, nothing in the universe was created back then, or would allow us to continue our current way of life today, or even enable us to improve or create more things for the future. Everything needed work before it reached fruition, and because everything was either work to be done, or work in progress, someone needed to do it. Thus, I will tell you the importance of work; the growth and the joy it can bring. With that said, if one does not work, neither should he eat, because all that he will be, if he does not work, is someone who will develop detrimental habits like taking things for granted, and also, on the extreme end, develop obesity. The world has nearly a billion people without sufficient food, and this is literally called "hunger," it is a different kind of hunger from the one that you will need to succeed in the world.

All creations, regardless of size, or shape, or color will go through at least some form of work. However, the interesting difference between a good and a great finished product is based on all that the product, commodity, or stock has gone through. And almost always, the tougher the work pressure, the greater the internal or external results that were produced. Internally, it could very well produce faster growth mentally, such as wisdom and understanding or the mental capacity to be alert after a long day, or spiritually it could produce results such as trusting God for help in ways not limited to physical strength, such as emotional strength to carry on after a tough loss in a relationship Externally, one would gain financial wealth, thus also increasing one's standard of living and quality of life.

In life, I believe that working is very important, and through working we grow. We become more mature in the way we speak, the way we think, and the way we handle things. I think one of the better ways to tell if someone is mature can be akin to someone who works out, think about it: if someone works out often, the most obvious thing to those around him would be the physical presence and the changes, he does not need to go around bragging about the weights he lifts nor does he have to flex or wear tight fitting clothes or clothes that reveals the muscles all the time, because it's easily visible even from afar! From the body shape, to the figure hugging T-shirt because it is only natural for the muscles to protrude out. It is the same even for maturity, though it is not physically obvious, but it can be "seen" easily.

As we come in contact with the various tasks given to us, they aid our growth. We pick up new skills, acquire more knowledge, and learn how to communicate with others. They help us to easily identify the areas where we have special talent and can excel, and those for which we are not well suited. And this makes our life easier in the future when it comes to contributing to our work place. By knowing our strengths we can concentrate more in that certain area, and at times this could save us from embarrassment.

For example, imagine asking a salesman, who has never cooked in his entire life, to take the job of a chef, and imagine asking the chef, who has never sold anything in his life, to take the salesman's job. One would probably slice his fingers instead of the lettuce, and the latter would likely be fired after one month on the job. Now, I am for learning new things, but you get the point.

Another aspect I love about working is that it alleviates or almost eliminates "small" issues of our lives. Think about laziness, being a busybody, being distracted and their relation to unhappiness. The very reasons why people have such issues are because they aren't busy enough with their work, or that they do not use much, or even any, of their physical or mental strength. (Now with that said, you will find out in later chapters how we can give our best, and how to not give away our precious lives, time, thoughts, and emotions.)

These people are the very same ones who not only spread ill-gossips complain about other people, compare their lives with other people thus causing unnecessary emotional burdens, lack concentration, and worse still, they blame other people for their unhappiness, and the worst part is that they themselves are still lazy! There are also reasons why some are happier than others. People who are focused on the things that they are doing have no time to talk about others in a nonsensical way such as, "Tom can't come close to me; look at all the things I've done, and see how he always lays around. I don't even understand why people like him can hang around for long. Do you know that many people hate him because of his attitude and character and more......." Think about it, not only does it waste your time, it affects your mood, and from then on things get worse. You'll lose your cool and those around you will feel the peripheral effects and then a fight will start. All this happens just because of the way you speak as a result of your unhappiness. Did you know that the optimal level of concentration is only 20 to 45 minutes and once you lose focus, it'll take you 20 minutes to get focused again? Think about the extra 20 minutes of rest you'll get or to enjoy doing the things you like. You could easily do a lot more things like exercising, showering, or eating.

The importance of our work comes from our daily jobs, because it brings us the food on our tables, the clothes that we get to wear and the money to pay our bills, and because we know we cannot survive without these things, we place a very high emphasis on our jobs. At least, that is what a normal responsible person would do. And very likely we will do whatever it takes, because it is our main source of income. And apart from all the physical goodies it can bring, I have noticed that it creates a sense of urgency among the people in a good way. Have you ever noticed the difference between the users of a shopping mall and those in a train station at a business district? One hogs the way of all the other users and at times makes it look as though they are the only users on it, while the other has people automatically lined up to one side and leaving the extra path as an express lane for those really in a rush. Wouldn't it be nice if people actually learn to not hog the escalator and have more courtesy even on a normal day?

I mean I have been in countless situations whereby the train door just shuts right on my face simply because I was delayed by people standing in my way and hogging the escalator. It annoys me to know that I have spent a good thirty seconds saying "excuse me," and the worst part is when inconsiderate couples or adults stand as idle as a painted ship upon a painted ocean! And what's more, react slowly when they know someone is in a rush, and still think that they have the right of way. Come on, you ain't the walking dead.

Though it is very likely that in whatever we do at work; the basic hands-on skills we use in our work place will almost never be used outside our office that is, unless we are cooks. Interestingly, our brains get developed and we end up being more alert to our natural surroundings, such as our awareness to people around us and how we can be sensitive to their feelings or be more active in helping out. All in all, working, to me, is the fastest way for one to grow up because at work we seldom get what we want, and, because our choices are limited, we have our backs against the wall, and we can either choose to fight for our own survival or sit back and watch how the world moves on without us and see how people abhor lazy people.

My favorite part of working is not working literally but rather the outcome it brings. Working helps widen your perspective and makes you see life differently, so when you talk with people it adds a variety of ideas formed from different lives and lives that are transformed as a result of different experiences. This diversity is responsible for making life more interesting.

TALK IS FREE, ACTIONS ARE COSTLY

Talk is not cheap, it is free, thus, you've probably seen or know someone who talks more than he works, and likely talks way more than he does anything. These people are also very likely to be seen lazing around with a lifestyle that is not fulfilling to themselves or others. Chances are it's because of the way they've been brought up. Ever heard the phrase "small people talk big, and big people talk small"? What this means is that one out of the two knows where, when, and how to put his brain, mouth and effort at the right place and right time, while the other is likely to have a non-present brain!

The most successful people are always "doing" way more than they talk, simply because they know that the more they talk it's more time wasted, and opens the door for more mistakes for others to point out – yes it's great to talk and joke around, but when it comes down to doing things, the successful people have already "left" the talk and are already on their way towards another goal. Also, because these people understand that mere talk will lead to poverty and would destroy their lives.

As for the one who talks and does nothing, it simply is an underlying truth that he is unable to back up his words with actions, thus; he does things cowardly by trying to cover up his flaws with more words. If people would actually learn and put actions into words, I'm very sure we'd hear more, "I did what I wanted to," and less, "I wish I had done something instead of wasting time." Think Hollywood movies—even the most successful Hollywood movies were all actions into words. The directors and actors took a story from a book, wrote a plot, and acted on the written plot. Though it sounds so simple, yet it's anything but simple, easy, or free. At the end of the day, everyone involved would have to put in their time, effort, and risk—these are the costly actions for a successful movie.

WORK ESSENTIALS.

The following are work essentials that I believe are the pillars of success in your work place, and the missing link many lack to get things done.

COMMUNICATION

The beginning of all great working partnerships; the core of every successful job, is not skills, but rather communication, something that many humans like to replace with skills, know-how, and the common excuse "ignorance is bliss." Why I say so is because, even if you lacked the skill (of course we are talking about general instructions, tasks and jobs, not like those of a medical doctor who needs both skills and knowledge), with proper communication, ideas and instructions can be passed down clearly for the completion of a job.

The most important aspect of communication is being on the same frequency; both the speaker and the listener have to be in line with each other. It sounds so easy, yet, for the weirdest reasons, a dispute or quarrel breaks out so often just because no one is on the same frequency. Think of the words that are spelled the same, for example the word "type." It could simply mean the number of words one can type on a keyboard within a minute, or it could very well mean that some girl isn't my type. But still there are words that are spelled differently yet sound the same but have different meanings for example, buy, and bye.

To back up my point, I'd just like to mention that, if and when the world is totally governed by robots then, for sure, the basic communication between humans can be abolished. Till then, we need to get back to the basics and continue to work on it. Without proper communications, the only thing that will happen is no-thing and misunderstanding; something that happens more often than one would think. For example, Sam asks James to follow up on a certain assignment and James follows through, but James, upon completing the task, failed to update Sam. And so Sam is left hanging to guess the outcome of the situation. Sometimes we often overlook the smallest detail because in our minds we think, "Sam should know that since James has agreed to follow up it means that everything will be fine," that is assumption – the cause of many issues. But in actual fact, Sam is lost in transition, and gets frustrated because he does not know the updates and is left waiting. Sometimes I think it would be great if we could just spare a thought for others and keep them updated, after all, it was a task given by someone and we should show accountability.

Even non-verbal communications such as body language and sign language are forms of communication! There is a general consensus that "communication is 55% body language or 93% nonverbal" and also there is the opposition that says it's a myth. Regardless of which side you think is correct, the main point of communication is simply to get your point across and understood without creating any annoyance or distorted information for others. Even if there should be any, it should not be often. I think the main reason why many companies are unable to be at their best performance level (minus the pride and ego issues) lies within the poor, if not vague, communication that leads to misinformation amongst workers, thus causing more issues like time wastage on repeating earlier information.

There are many ways to get your point across, with many more ways to either make or break a deal, or allow others to decide whether you should be in their good or bad books. Though it's good to put things across nicely, that is, what you say, a greater emphasis must be placed on how you say things. The best communicators are aware of and sensitive to the power of thoughts and emotions communicated nonverbally. Personally, I prefer to communicate up front, face-to-face, especially if it concerns something very important, as information could easily be lost, stolen, or tweaked along the way; also, because through one's body language and speech you could easily tell whether they are lying, angry, or inattentive.

The one thing I know of great leaders is that they are great communicators – they are open and straightforward. The start of good communication is when one is open and not afraid to speak his mind. Great leaders are also able to deliver their points across in a way that is easily understood by others. Something I think we all can learn to do is to go down to the level of the listener—this shows empathy, and it will draw more people to you. Making yourself sound impressive when no one understands you, is like getting angry with your own mirror image for being you.

But really, communication goes both ways. As much as it is important to get your point across, heard, and understood. It's sad that many times great communications do not happen because both parties—not just one, have refused to listen, therefore destroying any planks for building the bridge.

Communication also includes transmitting the right things. I remember how I got into an ugly mess with a colleague just because someone transmitted half of my points to the recipient without giving the whole story. And sometimes it is hard for the recipient not to be angry, either, because the recipient's mind has run wild with imaginations. Imagine hearing only "Well, this guy's priorities are wrong, he's wasting his time and he really shouldn't be working outside, because it's affecting his contribution." What do you think is running through his mind? Of course, anger, cursing, and swearing with personal attacks. Think about it, had the recipient heard the subsequent line, "...but maybe he has some serious family issues that's why he has to work, though. I feel for him, because it's really tiring."

But still, I need to point out that sometimes it's better talking to a wall than to people who are likely to cause unnecessary sparks.

Towards mending a sore relationship: I think being open and patching things up quickly would work. But, of course, the main issue standing in our way is usually our pride, but the longer we prolong patching things up, the emptiness and uneasiness will greatly increase, and there will be a larger sense of awkwardness. The longer it takes, the more pressure will build up.

The last thing about communication that you rarely hear about, is asking questions. Asking questions shows that you may have a wider perspective than the presenter; it also allows you to clarify your doubts and show others that you are not afraid of standing up. But of course, one's got to ask intelligently.

TRUST

Now that you've gotten your points across, what you need next is trust. Within trust, we find the word *US;* it means that two people must be on the same page. Trust could be like a tissue paper to one and a gold bar to another. The former abuses trust and treats it as something cheap and disposable, whereas the latter is very cautious when it comes to handling his gold bar. One weighs some 10-35 Grams per square meter, while the real deal weighs 12.4 kg. Guess who wins in a fight? But the truth behind it is that the gold bar has gone through a much longer and tougher process; through refining we get something more valuable and lasting, and the appreciation value increases with time. Apart from the gruelling time difference, the physical properties already differ—one gives way too easily, the other doesn't.

You could liken someone who is quick to backstab you for gains that only benefit him as a piece of tissue paper because he gives way too easily. While you could also liken someone else as a gold bar because he refuses to betray trust for a moment of pleasure because he understands that real trust cannot be bought by money but must be gained (even though money could make a difference in terms of making a deal happen). Only the corrupt man accepts a bribe in secret so that he may pervert the ways of justice to soothe his poor soul.

Trust starts with transparency; have you ever been in a conversation or presentation with someone when, despite hearing all the good reports, you feel a sense of uneasiness and have more doubts, even as more good results are spoken concurrently? Why? It is simply because you do not trust the person, and also because the person fails to be transparent with his answers towards your concerns, and evades or covers them up, if possible. Generally, mankind has often believed that by being transparent one shows weakness, but, on the contrary, so often we find people who are transparent with themselves and their struggles, have built the strongest bond of trust. I am not saying that you should go around selling out your flaws and shortcomings, but showing and being transparent at the right time makes all the difference in the world.

Trust is a substance. It cannot be seen or felt physically, but mentally, emotionally, and spiritually you know it is there. Very likely it is formed over time, through working together. The best way is when two people who have their backs against the wall are fighting together for survival. As it takes two hands to clap, so does it take two hands to build trust; not your own pair of hands but one of yours and one of the other person's. Trust is born when one party first believes in the other party, and then the latter has to seal the deal by backing up his words with actions. Trust exposes itself for what it is, and someone who really trusts you will by no means have any doubts or plans to harm you or to turn around and bite you.

Trust has three pillars supporting it: self-integrity, honesty, and tolerance.

Self-Integrity - Self-Integrity is not a code word; it is not pure talking, rather, it is pure action that relies heavily on self-respect. If one has self-respect, his integrity will show and back his actions up. Self-integrity comes from a belief, a belief in one's self. It is nothing more than just what you believe in; at the same time it is reflected in your conduct. It is just like your body wash, if the soap is of a good scent, you don't have to tell people about it, because it can be smelled from afar. To me, your Grammy-award-winning speeches like "trust me," or "Don't worry, I would never backstab you," does nothing for me until I have seen that both your actions and words come hand in hand. But then, now you'll say, "Oh, is there no room for mistakes?" Making mistakes are normal and forgivable, but the tracks leading up to the intention play a major role. Did he have a motive? Was it deliberate? I always believed that an untrustworthy one, regardless of his eloquent speech, will give away his despicable ideas through his speeches. It is very likely that, by the mid-way point in his speech, his conscience will have bitten him, thus causing him to fall off the beaten track. Trust not in his worthless speech, but you will be able to tell by the fruits of his words and actions whether someone will, or has compromised his integrity. Integrity is being real with oneself.

Honesty - Honesty is very expensive. Cheap people will never be able to afford it. Coming to terms with someone is actually one of the hardest things in life because the truth hurts. Honesty is very important when it comes to building trust. You need to be open to others so that they may know where you are coming from and can better help you. Still, it all starts by being honest with yourself and knowing that you need help. There is a reason why fake people only take things, and very often they take so many things that things starts to fall off their hands one at a time till they are left with nothing. All this happens because they do not trust others. To these people, the most painful thing is their own self-reflection, because all they have is the makeup to cover up their dishonesty. But, once makeup touches water it smudges. How will you want to look? As a reflection off the mirror? As someone "covered" and liked for who you are not? Or as someone real, and loved for who you are, even though you may get fewer likes? I think it is all right to say that you do not know the answer to certain things. In truth and fact, no one knows the answers to everything. Consider, for example, a question made by a customer with regards to your product. Personally, it is better to admit your flaw than to give an answer that is not even close. By doing so, you're only going to get yourself into more trouble. I'd rather deal with someone who is open, straightforward, and honest, because more than anything, it tells me about your character.

Tolerance - Tolerance is respecting where the other person is coming from. All of us have different views, knowledge, and different levels of understanding. It takes a lot of giving and moving on but it is certainly hard work. Working on commitments takes time and effort, and it may not always work out, but once you know the level of authenticity of the other persons it makes things much easier. That is when you decide if you should continue trusting them or not.

The level of trust differs to various degrees amongst different people. Many times people build trust based solely on their past experiences and use it as a measuring stick for the current situation. It's like using your own master key to open up all the doors, sometimes it works, but more often than not it doesn't. So the thing about trust—or, for the matter, when you have someone's trust do not treat it lightly. You can have a million gold bars, but if you treat each gold bar like it is replaceable, then do not be surprised if the world runs out of gold for you one day.

I think trust that is built between two people who understand that their relationship is more important than any single outcome is something very worthy and notable. When trust is engaged with the right people at the right time, your invisible world almost instantly become invincible

SKILLS AND UNDERSTANDING

There are things that are good to have but are not necessary, and there are things that are a "must-have." We all have a brain; at least it's physically present even if you do not use it. With that said, I think it is good to know whether you are a left-brain dominant or a right-brain dominant person, but a must-have for me would be to continue working on whatever skill-set that I have, and that I am already good at and also to work on developing new skills.

There are three types of skills when it comes to work; hard, soft, and transferrable. Or it could be an overlap of both, hard skills are likely to be learned during our school lessons: the ones that do not change over time and are fixed throughout, and require more of the left brain. This means that these people, the left brain dominants, will use more of their IQs, analytical, and logical skills for their job, and are likely to be, but not limited to, an accountant, an engineer, or a scientist, or a paralegal.

On the other hand, soft skills are likely learned outside of the classroom and based on things that are constantly changing and are not fixed, like dealings with people; these people are right-brain dominant and will use more of their EQ or Emotional Intelligence for their jobs and are likely to be, but not limited to, a chef, a counsellor, a designer, or a motivational speaker. (I believe at the end of the book you'll find out if I am a left or right brainer).

Then there are also jobs that are a mixture of both. One example of a job that uses more hard skills and lesser soft skills is a lawyer; simply because he needs to know the statutes well, as well as communicating to his client. The opposite of the lawyer's profession is the one which uses more soft skills and lesser hard skills which might be a sales person, as his main focus is to persuade the customer to buy his product with a little knowledge of the product.

Then there are transferrable skills also known as portable skills that we have learned along the way throughout our lives and at work. Such skills include: communication, leadership, organisation, numeracy, IT knowledge, time management, teamwork, and more. These skills allow us to make our job easier by aiding us with the knowledge that is required indirectly. For example, an engineer may spend 95% of his time dealing with machines and the remaining 5% to talk to his colleagues who, just like him, do not mind his language. But because he has to make a sales pitch, a presentation to his client, he now has to work on his communication to ensure that he carries the right attitude and tone when communicating among other relatable skills. To me, these skills are often underrated simply because people often think of work as a one dimensional pyramid, choosing to overlook the smaller less prominent edge. It is like your eye saying to your fingers "I have no need of you especially since I can afford to lose one." Trust me; if you do it to one finger you'll do it to the other nine! The point is that having more skills will only benefit you. But if you say to yourself, "This and that isn't important to know or learn and it's not worth my time," then you've shut the door of growing and improving on yourself.

There is a verse in the Bible that teaches us how and when to use certain skill-sets of which is also one of my favourite, It says *I know how to be brought low, and I know how to abound. In any and every circumstance, I have learned the secret of facing plenty and hunger, abundance and need. (English Standard Version, Philippians 4:12).* I would say that people need to learn this secret transitional skill; it is a great addition to both our hard and soft skill sets. It teaches us how to carry ourselves when we are faced with or put in different situations especially when it relates to money and relationships. I believe that the Bible with thousands of manuscripts which does not contradict itself could be trusted.

I feel that soft skills are more important than hard skills, because soft skills are not easily learned. They require more face-time with people than hard skills which are almost all based on memory work the majority of the time. With soft skills alone, you could still talk your way through, but if you rely on hard skills alone it is harder, as you are constrained by your limited knowledge to get you through people. (And for the fact, humans are not dead)

The one thing about the working world is that it is heavily dependent on pure paper qualifications. Companies hire people just based on certificates, thinking that humans are like machines, largely ignoring the simple fact of the importance of workplace culture, and the understanding of employees and their personal "touch." While the gears of different machines can be easily integrated, humans may not, would not, and may never integrate as easily as these machines do. It is very easy to change a gear every now and then, but with humans it will never be the same. Finding people with qualifications is easy, there are thousands of graduates each year with different majors, PhD and more from different faculties. It is like looking for a Koi fish in a Koi pond filled with Kois. I mean considering how the world has placed an extremely high value on certificates and qualifications, we seldom hear people talking about the importance of how it is for employees to work well together. I understand that people come and go – I generally believe that if someone walks out on me it's their loss, however it is also important to retain the right people. With that said, I believe that bosses should defend righteousness, not age. This means that there should be no such thing as the explanation, "He's young, that's why."

One reason why tribes are strong enough, in terms of trust and cohesiveness when fighting a war is simple—Tribal leaders focus on building up the tribe. It means to improve the tribal culture. Should they be seen as successful, the tribe would give their best, and this includes loyalty, but I believe that more than anything it starts with building a relationship, and once people know you are a talent magnet, people will be drawn to you and want to work for you and with you.

To me, I think a great leader is someone who would hire an employee by considering the individual's compatibility with the current work culture of the office first, before considering the paper qualifications. (Of course, the paper qualifications are important, yet strangely enough many are doing jobs that are not related to their field of study) because finding someone who shares the same mind-set, align their goals, vision and mission of the company is so much harder as to hiring someone with the exact paper qualifications you want, but what companies need are people like the former.

The personal "touch" of an employee or co-worker makes a huge difference especially if the employee is someone who has influence over his peers or with his superiors. Sometimes it is not about the position but the individual himself.

I feel that there isn't enough effort put in by both employers and employees to understand each other apart from the job requirements itself. Everyone is unique and everyone works differently, understands things differently, and communicates differently, and has different skill sets. So often we have companies using a "one-size-fits-all" method, and then, when they get poor results from the trainings, they blame employees for being incompetent. Sometimes it is actually much more simple and cost effective when people just sit down to talk and understand each other, and understand where each of them is coming from. Not only will the expectations be set out, but it will also help to identify the best way and place for the employee to work and thrive in. It will certainly help if bosses observe the way the employee works and then, from there, decide how best to help him. Getting to know him or her background certainly helps, because, apart from work, we all have other life issues to deal with such as family and financial issues, both of which I'd say are more important than work. It is just that work takes up more than half of our time.

Many bosses often use the cheapest excuse to free themselves instead of helping out.

They'd say things like, "you guys better solve this or one or both will get fired," or maybe the "nicer" boss might say, "well, you're grownups, so it wouldn't be nice if I interfered." While every other company is gunning for results, especially in such times where uncertainty is the only certainty, why not give yourself an edge by working on your employee's skills and understanding? Since all are grownups, then be mature enough to sit down, talk face-to-face, and do not pull off a child-like attitude by making personal attacks or bringing up non-related things such as past issues. If both have a problem, deal with the problem, not the problemer! (Problemer here refers to the person).

This is proof of a great boss. Because he cares enough for the individual, and much more about the relationship than the job. Again this is a great way to build trust and would certainly motivate the individual to work harder, and, then again, the company would reap the benefits!

Procrastinating Versus Pacing

Whenever it comes to work, it always seems like some people enjoy and need the rush factor to awaken their minds to start working. And yes, at times it seems as though such people are the ones who do better, however, this method would not work in the long run. Certain workers think that, "If I could study at the 11th hour and still get grade A, why not at work too?" You see, in school, regardless of how many assignments you are given by your teacher, it is all part of a fixed work plan for the year. On top of it, many teachers do not want to be tied down by endless marking. Therefore, they themselves have a limit on the school workload. But because many people with such a mind-set are often oblivious, or rather, choose to think that the probability of something extra occurring along the way is near zero, hence they choose to procrastinate. The truth about work is this – the faster you run away from completing a task, the quicker it catches up.

Unless you are in an industry that makes or sells things that are built to order, then it would be of almost no concern to you, because you can only work when there's an order placed, but then again, how many jobs are created specifically like that? Even a financial adviser, who has the flexibility of a whole year to reach his target, deems that he needs only to work six months a year on average to achieve his target, and so he starts off at the second half of the year while enjoying the first half of the year procrastinating, believing that he is so good that maybe he does not really need the six months, but maybe only needs three months. So he procrastinates further, after wasting an extra three months he finally starts. But when he starts working the economy suddenly melts; no one wants to buy his product and no one has referrals for him. Suddenly more personal issues such as health and relationships appear out of nowhere, and he is forced to stop working for some time and now he feels the heat. (But then you'll say, oh Kieroy, you really do not understand how much money I have made throughout my years in this industry, so much so that I can retire anytime). Do not be shallow-minded, if you have enough money; (Although I know for a fact that there is no one who has enough money; even billionaires are concerned daily about how to bring in more income to maintain their lifestyle, or to ensure that their wealth does not dwindle overnight) you would not be feeling the heat to achieve your target.

Procrastinating is like an addictive drug, once you start you can't stop, so don't start.

I don't enjoy procrastinating, or maybe some would say that I can't chill and thus am always in a hurry to do things—the total opposite of procrastinating, but I tell you this, smart people prepare to be ready before things happen and do the necessary things first as opposed to doing things only when they're needed. (Yes, I understand that not all things can be prepared for, but neither should we use it as an excuse to laze around). Call it a rushing disorder or whatever, at least I'm better prepared—at the end of the day great players all work on hitting that one game-winning shot for the championship.

Retrospectively, of course, we hope to be the total opposite of procrastinators—proactive as much as possible. However, so many people get burned out from work because they do not pace themselves for the long run. Though giving one's best daily sounds great, let's be realistic—even a car that goes on fifth gear all the time will eventually break down faster. I think there are days whereby we could push a little bit more, and then there are days where we should just cruise at the third gear. There's no glory if you win the first three rounds but end up losing the race cup because your engine requires an overhaul. I know that there are times to grind it out; to persevere till the end, but quick power breaks are the reason why people can work at a higher level of intensity and produce better results. Even machines have downtime to rest, how much more should you do it?

Everyone has different workloads, so even though it is impossible to have a one size-fits-all method, I think being selective in doing whatever is the most important first and then canceling out things that are less important makes a huge difference. Life is a marathon, even though at times it somehow seems to look like a short distant sprinting event, especially when we think that with every yearly exam or job assignment it is a one-off race to the finish line, but it isn't a sprinting event because life is worth much more than your work. Sprinting takes up more energy and causes your body to break down faster as compared to a longer distance where the body breaks down but at a slower pace. The race in life, I think, would always be an endurance race—a race to see the last man standing. But you still have to start somewhere, because time disappears and never comes back.

WORK ETHIC AND THE LACK OF IT

Work ethic is a habit; money can buy you almost everything except a habit. Work ethic brings consistency which is needed if you want to be at least good at something for a very long time. And consistency is an ongoing process of maintaining your current work ethic. I think one of the hardest things about work ethic—consistency, is that, because it becomes so mundane, people give up after a while, either because they see no results, or are happy with where they are. Just look at people who work out just for the sake of doing it, just because a beach party is coming up. So they go hard for 1 month and then slack off totally after the event. Therefore, these people only have a "basic" body shape, nothing too fancy as to those who consistently work out. I'm not talking about professionals but even average day-to-day people. Or else they'll be on the other end, giving up after 3 months, just because they don't see many results. If you know you'll quit early, my advice is not even to start.

Every time I think about the phrase "work ethic," I always think of the scientific equation $E = mc^2$. This special equation can be used to relate the total energy to the total mass, and in order to find out how much energy an object has we multiply the mass of the object by the square of the speed of light; we multiply because when mass is converted into energy the resulting energy is defined by the moving speed of light. Pure energy is electromagnetic radiation; just like light which is an electromagnetic wave that's experienced and visible to all. Work ethic requires an individual to bring forth energy. This means it is impossible to be lazy and claim to have a good work ethic. Just as you cannot see electromagnetic radiation, but you know that it is there, the most glaring thing about having a good strong work ethic is that, unconsciously, it gives off a sense of attractiveness to those around you. Also, we may consider the formula of kinetic energy $1/2 \ m \ v^2$ thus causing a small object to produce a large amount of energy about 448,900,000,000,000,000 in units of mph. This tells me that in life, it's never about the size of your obstacle but the size of your will and drive to be an obstacle-slayer.

Sadly, there is something about the current generation that I feel is in shortage of —work ethic; don't get angry if you are part of the Gen-Y group, for I am in the same Generation, just with a different explanation, and besides, if you're offended, trust me, I've already hit the jackpot because chances are when someone shares something which makes you feel offended there's probably truths to it. As the years go by I think the meaning of work ethic seems to dwindle down with every passing generation. It seems like hunger can be found anywhere and everywhere else, except when it comes to work. You could hunger for food, hunger for the latest fashion craze, hunger for the latest IT products, but just not work. I think the phrases "a lack of hunger" and "overly-protected" sum it all up. (I know all of us are guilty to various degrees of feeling a sense of entitlement, but really, if you have a majority of the weight scaled towards feeling that everything in life is an entitled compliment, then shame on you. And it is also very likely that if you feel that everything is an entitlement, you are likely to be poor at giving, selfish and unappreciative towards people. Not too many people understand that whatever we have now is only temporary, but what we give to others may spark off a lifetime of giving in their own life. By giving, it makes others fond of you as well. Who doesn't like treats?

Everything boils down to how much people are exposed to, not a matter of richness or poorness but how much one is exposed to; because seeing someone work their butt off just to pay the bills would really blow your mind away if you think that money drops freely from heaven. Not richness because there will always be rich spoiled brats who are lazy and then there are also the esoteric rich people who have kids who are dead hardworking and would not mind getting their hands dirty instead of sitting down in their cosy living room, because these kids understand that things in life do not come easy; neither are things of the fantasy world real. If you are rich, but if you also know that your riches did not come easily you would work even harder to ensure that it grows or at least does not dwindle down over time. These people also believe that real pleasures of life come not by misusing riches that are passed down to them but by working hard and grinding each and every "brick wall" that stands in their way so that they may complete their tasks at hand or move towards their goals. This is the exact explanation as to why some kids do not mind sweating under the sun working for his/her own father - simply because only those who are secure internally do not have problems with giving their all. It's easy for such people to put down their pride; to do the "dirty" jobs to get things done because they know they have been given all things in life. On top of it, if you quickly put down your pride and get something done, it makes things easier, because the longer you delay; your pride rises with every passing second. Having this skill—ethic, says a lot about your character. A skill engraved within is yours to keep forever. And it is attractive to bosses for they will overlook your peers and zero in on you. But the opposite holds true as well—if you are lazy; no one wants to work with you, let alone want to know you. Hard work is the bridge from dislike to respect. People may hate you, but they have to give you the much deserved respect for the work you put in. The key is this—if you come in ready to work, right from the start, then a lot of minor issues will work out by itself.

Riches do not bring work ethic, but work ethic might bring riches. Talented, smarter, better-looking people are aplenty, but plenty do not bring the energy and effort to outshine the talents, smarts, and looks that will fade away like vapour.

In essence, I think that it is always more fun and challenging to bake your own bread from pure flour as to buying it off the shelves – starting from scratch, you will never know what you find, learn or get along the way that could be the start to something new or improved. Though you may not have as many materialistic things compared to friends whose parents give them everything, but certainly you would be shocked if you realized that they lack mature intellectual intelligence when it comes to life and work. These experiences that you get out there from working makes you see that in life, happiness does not always dwell in physical material goods and that understanding things in life is way more satisfying to one's soul. Not always is anything that glitters gold, nor are things that are seen always real.

It seems like people these days, especially kids, are always awaiting the "right time" or "right condition" before they actually start working. What is the right time? They will tell you things like "oh, when I reach a certain age," or "when my friends start working," or "when the never-ending television series ends." Or else they will say the right condition will be, "when I feel like it is time to work." Or worse still, they may even end up saying, "I do not want to work here or there because it sucks," or they'll say, "Because my friend says so." Don't be a fool, or even a fool like your friend. For all you know they are discouraging you from working but are working themselves, so that they may gain not only more money but more experience in life, and you also end up shutting the door on learning and experience. The bigger truth that your "friends" could not tell you or do not want you to know is that – it'll be one less competition for them. A real friend is one that helps you grow, not stunts your growth. Take my advice, hang out with eagles and soar, not eat dirt like chickens running around in circles. But, sadly, the right time and condition for many only occurs when they want it to, and when and how they think that things should happen. The thing is—the chances of a right condition rarely appear in our lives, but only with the right mind-set, then only will our conditions turn right. But even if they start working, do not be too quick to say, "Oh, she's a grown-up now, and she's finally working." It's simple because most of the time kids start off with much enthusiasm just so they can please their parents, or simply to just stop the parents' ranting for them to start working. Maybe these kids are motivated to work just so they can buy something that they want – and that is not wrong, but I'm sure what you'd like to see more often instead would be for them not to only have the things they want in life to enjoy, but to also be wise with their hard-earned money.

Motivation gets one started, but a habit keeps them going, and that is why this topic is all about having a good work ethic. There are so many countless things in life that adults have to pay off with their salary and kids know nothing about it, but even if they knew about the need to pay off the daily expenses, they never understand how tough it is to actually go out there and bring the money back for the family. But one thing I know about waiting for the right time; it never happens in life but almost certainly I can tell you – come harvest time, the slacker will look on hungry without food, because when it was time to work he did not. Speaking about motivation, you know you have a strong work ethic when you're self-motivated more often than not, and it gets you frustrated that you cannot work or finish your task because you're down with an injury or illness. And it annoys you more than anything, even more than the pain caused by your illness that you can't work, because you know that precious time is slipping away.

"GET A LIFE!"

Have you ever been told to "get a life!"? I got it a couple of times from kids who thinks that their life revolves around playing games, having fun and work is nothing but for adults. Well whenever some kids tell me that I do not waste my time to even acknowledge their presence let alone reply them, but I do pity them for being naive and dumb, it's a different kind of naive that people use to say "babies are so naive," I think even babies have more intellectual awareness than the kid who runs his big mouth over such things.

When I say kids, I mean people who have outwardly reached the age of maturity yet behave as though they do not have it; maturity does not come with age, it is the exposure and understanding of things that brings maturity. Someone could be twenty-six years old and you could say that they are still kid-like; it is not a party environment whereby you'd say, "be young at heart or bring out the kid in you," but really just the maturity level. Other times I'd think of and allude to an eighteen-year-old as a mature young adult because they display qualities when it comes to work; namely maturity and understanding. Working doesn't help a kid grow much, unless they are solely reliant on themselves, because working and getting allowances from parents at the same time will only bring one to a certain level, but to go higher, the kid has to stop taking allowances then they will really grow up and understand how tough it is. For an example, if they are paid $5 an hour would they be willing to splurge $10 on a cup of coffee? To put things into better perspective, do you think they would spend lavishly on a phone that would cost them $800? If they are of the right mind, they'll know that it takes them two hours to earn a drink and only twenty minutes to finish it or even months to earn a phone. That is if they do not get any extra money for their drink from their parents.

Because the extra money earned while getting allowances won't accelerate your growth; it's like swimming with a lifesaving float in the Dead Sea and saying that you can swim well! And if you do not know, people are able to float easily without wearing a float in the red sea because of the seawaters' high salinity. Having responsibilities makes one more responsible and mature; I think that is why people who have no responsibilities often show up with the worst attitudes.

Even so, at times I feel that one of the biggest contributors to kids who have such lazy, spoiled and laid -back attitudes is because parents often have a veil of being too protective over their own kids, and each time a kid throws a fuss, they would quickly give in so as to stop the nuisance act. But if you do it right the first few times when they are at a tender age; by not giving in all the time, then there won't be a next time in the future. Once they reach a certain age or point in their lives, all your efforts to try and show them the importance of working will only be seen as a nagging.

I believe that there is a place for encouragement, for having a time frame for growth, but there is a limit to it. But if you do not stand firm with them when you're supposed to, it's normal for them to see that not only are you indecisive, but your words lack power. Yes, there are great results in encouraging them and I certainly know that it is a way that the younger generations are more accustomed to. However, if you were never strict with them, then no one will ever be able to differentiate the two different ways. The most effective way for encouragement to work is to first have a standard of firmness, and then, when you add on encouragement the result is way better than having only one of them. Still, it depends on the maturity of the child, encouragement can do great wonders regardless of age but using it at the right time makes a world of difference. That is, considering the fact that you deal with them correctly right from the start, that they may know that discipline can do them much good. Be it at work or even when dealing with others, they will still have good manners.

By doing so, by saying no; and by not giving in all the time, you are indirectly preparing them for life in the real world, and it is so much more important because, normally, a parent will not outlive the child and the child would also grow up to know that out there in the world no one is going to give anyone anything let alone everything, it's got to be earned. So then what happens when the parents are long gone? Now that is the real problem because the parents will not be around to help, but because the kid grew up getting everything he wanted, he will bring this "I don't care about anything; as long as I put on a childish act I will get anything I want, because people are going to give in to me eventually."

Let us now put the kid aside and talk about yourself. I'd like to ask, how did you grow up to be a strong adult; someone mature and hardworking? Did it happen by chance or was it because you went through certain tough times in life that made you who you are today? It's okay I know the answer. But if your answer was, "Well I had everything easy in life," then it's better for you to burn this book right away because certainly, your child will not walk the same path as you. Going back to your children, giving in all the time is like feeding their habits and encouraging them to repeat the same old antics time and time again. On your part, even if you knew the proverb about training up your child in the way that he should go so that he will not turn away from it when he's old, it is useless 'cause it's only head knowledge, but not put to use. Head knowledge is dead without practice, have you forgotten to be a doer? But blessed are you who seek the truth, and are not offended because of it after reading this.

I know part of your pain; your difficulty and wanting to "throw them out" on the streets to let them grow. I love to play with kids, and I can only play with them; and scolding them is near impossible because we all know they are meant to be loved. But if we do not let them grow, they will lose out. Do not worry, it is only through "falling" then do they grow. No strong individual has a perfect record of not messing up. But it is when we try to keep things perfect, we lose not only the chance to grow, but also deprive others of growing. The degree to which you are exposed to setbacks, either mentally or physically, will shape your "core" the mind. Things do not change with time as the world always says, but rather it is the change of your mind, your perspective that changes things.

I believe that if kids experience failures and setbacks while growing up, or even at a young age it'll only strengthen them. But of course parents play a huge role. At times the risks could be controlled by parents, but at other times it's impossible. However, through it, a little bit of growth is added on, and their resilience mechanism will not only come in place early, but as they grow it will sharpen up. At time same time, it's paramount that parents also aid their growth in bouncing back from failures. Take bread as an example, while all bread are mainly made from flour, it is interesting to note that before flour becomes fine and soft, it is actually grounded before it plays the major role in contributing to a nice smelling hot bun fresh out of the oven.

We all worry about kids running with the wrong crowd and getting into all sorts of trouble with the law. Still, it seems like one of the best ways to handle such things with a positive side effect is to actively expose them to work; hard work. When they know how hard it is themselves and are also busy working for their own spending it reduces the energy to mess around, makes them wiser with their company of friends, and with handling money. Maybe they might still run with the wrong crowd at the start, but, in the long run, they would want to hang out with people identical to themselves – people who don't mess around and are hardworking. Because once you've turned the corner it's impossible to go back; the feeling is gone, and so they have moved on from their immature ways.

The way I look at and define $E = mc^2$ is: Ethic = mind-set and commitment and concentration. Why? It's simple, because I know that even though I may not be the best out there in every category or above anyone else, but I can still make a difference: I'm willing to learn, and I can do things that people can't or are unwilling to do. It's not about the people who say the things you can't do, or the black list of things that they force you into. It has nothing to do with who you are, or what you are, or where you come from, but it is a choice to just do it.

MIND-SET

The thing that gives victors the edge when it comes to succeeding at work, or even before they embark on the task at hand, always starts inside their head. You could say that they have a "victory before the battle" mind-set. Having such a mind-set is not living in denial nor does it mean that the person has no fear or doubt. But rather the person has a birth of confidence that will be evident and the gist of the "Victory before the battle" mind-set is about believing in yourself. Such a mind-set is the gold that fools can only talk about, but victors work to obtain it – no one is born with it. Only by working towards it does one then obtain it.

As humans we all have varying degrees of mental fears and flaws, we're afraid that things might not work out or are afraid that we might make the wrong choices and even afraid to fail. But each time we let our minds harbor such mental thoughts we're only bringing ourselves to defeat. We only have one life; why not give our best to have the best thoughts possible? It is not like we can reset our lives or we can predict the future. But all I know is that I'd rather do what I have to and can do now and maybe regret a little than to totally regret the fact that I wasted my life on things that made me moved over from doing something great and big just because something small was standing in front with a sign that says "you can't because I'm here." You know it's like seeing a huge shadow and thinking "this scares me, of how much more the actual thing?," when in fact it's just a tiny dog.

Failure, embarrassment, and sometimes humiliation are the last things on a victor's mind, not that these things aren't there, but somehow these victors are able to "blind" themselves from all these distractions, thoughts, and emotions. I believe that most victories are won long before they are fought, because the greatest fights happen behind closed doors while they are preparing themselves for a bigger stage. All this is only possible because they are focused: locked in, and ready to "kill." They do not spend time worrying about others (even if they do, it's minimal) but rather, they spend the most time on the current situation, and some time on the final results.

Then you'll ask, "How does one get such a mind-set?" Actually, it's rather simple: for me, whenever it comes to work the mind-set that I think is important to have, or at least, try to have is an all-out effort; this means you give your best in whatever you do, it's not about trying to be the best out there, but the best of the "best you." And besides, if someone pushes you, you can only go a certain distance before he/she gives up on you, but if you push yourself, you'll go to places farther than what you've ever expected! Everyone wants to be a victor, yet only few are called victors because of the work they put in.

Victors always have resilient minds; they do not crumble when they get rejected. They may get knocked down seven times, but they get up eight times.

COMMITMENT

Once you've developed the habit of having the right mind-set; that work ethic is nothing more than just making work a habit, then being committed comes naturally. Because it becomes a part of your life, see it this way; if you really love someone, going the extra mile seems seamlessly easy as compared to going the same extra mile for someone you dislike. At the end of the day the commitment comes easy when you love what you do—even sacrifice which is needed comes naturally. Also, your commitment is also upheld by your punctuality—are you always late? Being held up once in a while is understandable; the train breaks down, a massive jam on the road or some last minute toilet emergencies, but being late consistently shows that you lack the mental ability to succeed. Then, of how much more do you expect to be a victor in battles? On top of it, it's hard for people to respect you, because you can't even respect them by at least showing up on time.

Working becomes easy for the diligent, but harsh for the lazy because they need to be pushed constantly and, more importantly, you will not be able to go even as far as to push yourself. For by pushing yourself, you will easily exceed both yours and others' expectations. And the best part is that you end up breaking new ground and go to places that you've never thought that you would ever be able to go.

Whenever it comes to commitment, it always seems that the people who are committed the most to their work are those who can dig down deep and just pull out whatever that is within them to get the job done. As much as I can write, I'd still have a hard time putting the description into words. It's like one of those things whereby you know that you know it's there, but you just can't put it into words because the actions are just overwhelming. Sometimes I think it's like a hidden gear that only those who give their all get to unearth. These days, because things come way too easily for some kids, they take things for granted, thinking that because it is here today that it will still be here tomorrow. They never prepare themselves for changes and because of it, they become lazy; they often idle around wasting their time, or they'd complain their time away saying that they are bored. And, for sure, you need no rocket scientist to tell you the horrifying results years from now. If they cannot stay committed to working hard or even keeping their day job, what makes them think that, if they were to switch jobs, or get another job elsewhere in another industry, or even their "dream" job, that they'd be committed?

CONCENTRATION

In this era whereby concentration comes and goes as easily as the wind it's so much easier to lose focus. Getting our minds to concentrate on one thing is already tough and then, when you add on all the distractions of the world like TV programmes, the bad news, the latest fashion craze to follow, the tweets and texts coming in every minute it seems like concentration is just a word.

I'd like to add in some spices to bring back ways that can help us all concentrate as much as we can - it's not a competition, but it's important to know that concentrating on the right thing at the right time will propel us into new heights. I'm not against technologies and the IT tools and the TV shows; after all, it gives us some knowledge and makes our life more efficient, but I usually reserve my time for more important things—things that can build me up in more than one way: physically, mentally, spiritually, financially, and intellectually. I'd certainly prefer to spend my time on things that make me happier and not the opposite. Like things that would not only cause me to get distracted from the task at hand but, more importantly, things that would make me lose my joy and disrupt my mood for the whole day. Thus far, these are the five principles I live by whenever it comes to getting things done and the results are great.

5 WAYS TO IMPROVE CONCENTRATION LEVEL

One thing at a time. Sounds cliché, but, yes, you don't have to make things complicated to get good results. It's all about time management. Face it, it's never possible to do everything every time and give your best. Be selective in the things which you give your 100%.

It will also be more efficient if you gave 100% of your energy and effort to selected individual tasks instead of trying to give a 110% all the time, it may work in the short run, but in the long run it will never last because you're not a robot but rather a human. Prioritize your schedules, do the most important thing first, but on some days, if you're feeling a little bit energetic and in a better mood, do things that you may find more challenging first. Why? It's simple, since you have to do it sooner or later, why not pick a day when your mood is better and work on it? At least by starting somewhere it'll get you farther. And the quicker you get used to it, the easier it becomes.

Just so you know, humans were not really made to multi-task. Though there are reports saying that one can actually multi-task up to four things, but it has been scientifically proven that multi-tasking actually decreases our efficiency by 50%. On top of it, switching from one task to another makes it hard to tune out distractions and can easily cause mental blocks that will slow down your progress; trying to be everywhere and you'll go nowhere.

Please do not tell me about the artists that you see performing on stage that play an instrument or two and sings at the same time. They are they— while you are you, brother!

Envision the end product.

What I like to do to make sure I'm doing things one at a time is to envision the final product or picture. This way, not only will it keep me motivated and going, but also, I'll be in my best form and it's easier when you have a vision in mind.

Today if you go for an eye test and your reading is 6/6 or 20/20 it's great. It would usually mean you have a good eye-sight, or rather Visual acuity (VA), but it does not always mean that a good vision is present all the time. Our eye-sight is determined by how much our naked eyes are able to see. And many times we're often limited by our own immediate circumstances because it's easier to accept things in-front of you as they are. However, if you have good vision, you'll be more appreciative but most importantly you'll understand that there are good things waiting to be discovered behind the blurred lens of life despite your circumstances.

So what is the difference between your sight and vision? Simply put: Sight is the ability to see the physical world while vision is the unusual competence in discernment or perception. With that in mind, your vision is not limited, for it knows no end with a positive perception of life. Years ago I remember watching a blind man on television driving with the aid of someone, but my point is this. This old man, despite his blindness, was able to drive despite being completely blind. How much more you and I who are able to see? At the end of the day it's not about your natural eyes and what you can see but "eyes" that are willing to look beyond the natural and strive and excel towards the vision of the mind! The danger only comes when you lose your vision, because without a vision you have nothing to look forward to and to work towards, and many of the human races today have perished mentally because they have long lost their vision towards life.

Personally, I'm bugged with Strabismus and Nystagmus but it's funny how people with perfect or better eyesight having issues "focusing" on things. I mean thinking about it makes me feel that sometimes people who are handicapped seem to be at an advantage because they keep pushing their limits.

Eating right.

The most important thing when it comes to working is to have common sense, something which is rare, certainly common sense will tell you that you should not work hungry or go too long without food. To add on, people who are constantly drained and tired should take a good look at the food that they're eating. Is your diet made up of oily, fried and high levels of sugar most of the time? If so, that would account for your sluggish demeanour. The excessive oils in food makes you feel "heavy and tired" easily while the fluctuating levels of sugar is the culprit that makes you go high one moment and low the next instant. For me, water is my favorite drink; not only does it hydrate me but it makes me rely less on sugary drinks and prevents my body from becoming dehydrated. Did you know that our body is 70% water? On top of that fruits are usually my natural source of sugar - healthy sugar that keeps me going and besides, it prevents constipation as well. (That's why some people have cute nicknames like Uranus!)

Taking power breaks.

Same concept as power naps - short and sweet, though it could be included but what I like doing is taking my busy mind off from something and putting it into somewhere else where my mind is still busy - this means the energy level does not drop but only a change of mental scenery. I know it sounds crazy but it works well for me, so after that short period of 15 minutes or so I'll go back into what I was doing previously. You could do some stretching or push-ups to keep your blood circulating or you could wash your face.

Right environment.

Do you always find yourself being distracted? Does the person beside you talk too loud so much so that it disrupts your thinking? If yes, go elsewhere. Do you find yourself checking your Face book account every ten minutes? If yes close your browser. Usually when I'm studying or working on a project I like to lock myself up away from people and noises. I'll leave my phone away from me, and I'll only work with people that are serious, not some junky who's just there to get quick answers and return the favor with nonsense. Do yourself a favor; if you have to leave your friends or skip some events do it, it might be tough at first, but when the results reflect off your hard work, then you'll know the importance of having a right environment.

HAVING A STRONG WORK ETHIC.

At the end of the day, having a strong work ethic starts by being disciplined, and is partly the reason as to why some people are consistent at bringing in results, whereas others make improvements that are negligible. (Sometimes in life, your work ethic cannot eradicate the impact of a recession). But somewhere along the way, and I'm very sure you've experienced this as well – then there are days whereby either the workload never ends or you're just too tired that even after you've completed your job you can't sleep. The only way out is to carry on and push through, because at that moment it seems like our brains are just so locked in, that we can't even shut it down. And, yes, the after effect of exhaustion doesn't help much by making you feel speechless as a result of your hard work.

WORKING THROUGH
A DRY SEASON

There will be seasons when you feel dry, whereby you do not feel like working but again it's a habit, and alone; can I tell you that you have just mentally scaled down the earth's population from seven billion to one? Being lonely and tired is a terrible thing, but as we all know though we have friends, our friends are also busy with their work and therefore might not be able to even talk with us on the phone. That is the best time for you to think of the finish line and endure towards it. Even so it would be great if you could sing your blues away. Maybe you think no one is watching you, and maybe you think it seems like a good time to slack off. But most of the times, its times like that that allows us to grow; because now we're doing something good, something right even when no one is watching, and it makes it easier to perform when people are around, in time surely the good results will show up unannounced.

Sometimes, though it may be only a season, yet it seems as though there are no other seasons apart from the long, tiring and depressing one. No matter how much passion you have, think you have, or profess to have, we have times where we feel like giving up. And what's worse is that as you read this you still feel discouraged, and nothing seems like it's improving. Take courage, be strong. You may be hard-pressed but you cannot be crushed. Why? Because if you were crushed, you'd be dead, and the fact that you're alive and reading this says that you still have a life waiting to kick the dust off your soiled boots. Growing up, and going through such seasons actually benefitted me, much more than I could have ever imagined, and this book is the result of all that I have gone through. If you endure through, then your endurance will create a strong character and character creates confidence towards life. Character is like a tea bag, you never know how strong it is until it touches hot water.

Take a diamond for an example; it is formed under extreme pressure and temperature. Even though all natural diamonds go through the same process, some are of greater worth and value than others. While all diamonds can be cut, only few have the "cut" or, as some may say - "a cut above the rest." Within the diamond industry, the primary focus is always on the cut of the diamond, it determines whether it is an excellent grade or just average. At the end of the day, quality diamonds are made individually, and, for sure, if they could speak they would tell you that it's extremely lonely, and the heat they go through is terrible, but because they know they are meant to sparkle they'd press on. How much character and confidence you'd like to have is yours to choose. But if I were you, I'd want to have a life brimming with attractive character and strong confidence.

THE SWITCH

I think it'll come to a point whereby your work ethic is already there, and it is no longer a matter of building your work ethic, but knowing when to use it. I think when you've really gotten to such a point, things become as easy as flipping on or off a switch – something natural. It's like a microwave, when it's not in use it stays cool, but when it gets switched on then you'll realize that it heats up real fast. Sometimes some people who have the best work ethic, may come off as laid back or may look sleepy at times when it comes to work, but do not mistake their calm demeanour as lazy. These people certainly have confidence in the things they do, and their confidence is not coincidental. It's like watching a stage performance, the only reason why these performers look cool and calm is because of the countless hours they put in to make their stage fright look almost non-existent. Its real simple – the more you work on something the more confident you'll get.

Personally, I have to admit that sometimes I have a hard time turning off my own switch, I've often gotten more than annoyed, rather angry whenever I'm so locked in, so focused on something and then someone would walk in and ask me for some kind of help or even offer me food, I become someone who has a short fuse. Someone who goes off easily, and usually it's my parents who comes in and asks me questions about how my day went and

I'll be like "okay just average, I'm busy" Or else, it'll be like, "why do you always have to come in and talk to me over things that are not important when you see me so focused and busy? Go out. If it's important then tell me, else it can wait" or something along those lines that aren't very nice to hear. I may come off or sound wise but, yes, I do make mistakes, and my "work ethic" gets the better of me sometimes, because all I want to do is just get things done, and done well. I don't care if I have to lock myself up or skip meals or throw my phone away.

Still, I love my parents. They're the ones who often offer to cook me a meal after I come home late from work and when the helper at home is asleep.

A BIG THANK YOU TO FORMER GENERATIONS

All that my generation has and will have with regards to work and life is all because of the harder work put in by the older generations. And this is something that no one can ever take away, or take credit for, nor should anyone, especially if they are younger and claim that they can replicate the same thing. It annoys me to even hear of it. One day I was talking to a friend about work ethic and the things that the former generations have done for us, and he boldly claimed without his brains that its easy stuff to work long hours, so I quipped back "you certainly have a great sense of humour. Please, give me a break and let me have the day off." But then I realized, maybe he was right, of course he could claim that working long hours are easy because it's likely his brain was coated with cobwebs.

Regardless how much hard work we put in, it still pales in comparison with what the former generations did. It's just that simple; they paved the way to get to us, and where we are now, then how can one say that we paved the way for them? It's impossible! Though I would consider myself a workaholic, I am nowhere near many people, especially those born in the 1960s and before. I remember working up to slightly above sixty hours a week, and I was really tired, but here was another man in his late fifties, racking up nearly seventy hours a week. He would even bring back his work. Typically he would come in at seven a.m. and then leave at nine p.m. on most days. On top of it he goes hard at his work on weekends, too. I would like to thank the older generations for the hard work put in, because it paved the way for people like me and also set the path for us to continue and so pass it down to the coming generations and then thereafter.

I got part of my work ethic from watching my own dad work, and it drove me to take things up another level myself. Growing up and watching my dad work relentlessly made me want to be like him, it's just so amazing. I wish kids would actually get out there and see their own parents at work – how hard they work just to put food on the table. The reason why so many kids lack the drive is because they were never exposed to such great stuff at an early age, and by the time they realize the importance it's difficult for them to cultivate such habits because it has become alien to them – something new, and because this "new" thing seems tough they shy away and shove it aside instead of embracing it.

Passing the world over to younger generations who lack a work ethic is a scary thought that is already unfolding before our eyes. The former generation worked so hard to make the world "spin" on its axis, but today, because too many youngsters lack the work ethic and drive to continue; to sustain and improve things, where the former generation will eventually pass the baton to. The world will collapse.

WHAT DID I JUST SAY?

I know after all this "drilling" about the importance of having a strong work ethic and having a serious attitude towards it, personally sometimes I feel like I perform better when I'm oblivious to my surroundings and even better if I do not know what I'm going into. My mind can be blank, and I look as though I have a stone-face, it's like my soul has left me. It's like sleep walking, but in this case it's sleep working. And then I wait until I get hit by reality before awaking. But it's an amazing feeling, even right now, writing this, I'm in a state of "sleep working." And things seem to flow much better.

I guess it's just about being open to anything, having a "whatever" mind-set at work so that you will not feel overloaded.

ATTITUDE THE PATH AND LEARNING THE WAY— NOT EDUCATION

Before I go into detail, I'd like to say up front that basic education is a must this means at least completing high school so that you may know the fundamentals of life and education has without a doubt allowed our minds to grow and be fattened intellectually. It has trained our minds to be sharper and quicker; by working on our memory skills.

If you are able to further your studies, go for it, but it should never be your main source of growth for life neither should it cause you to be high on education, moderate on learning and treating the less educated lowly. Education is meant for a good cause, it is meant to educate people for good and the sole purpose of education to me – is to make the world a better place. Though is it easier said than done, forcing kids to study will not work in the long run and will certainly back-fire. Every kid's attention span differs greatly, gauge it, then use it to plan the best way possible on encouraging the kid to learn, like I said with work ethic—it is a habit, do it right the first few times and then subsequently things get easier. Do not always allow them to play first before studying, do it the other way around. This way they will develop a mind-set such that they need to work before they are allowed to play. (Of course let them play without any reminders of how much work they are left with, because this, in turn, will ingrain in them a never-relaxed mind-set, which is bad in the long run. Chances are, as they grow up, even while having fun on the outside, mentally they are thinking about the leftover homework and dreaming about it. How then can you say that your child has a proper childhood?)

Attitude is like an optical illusion; it looks different from every angle, yet it is physically seen and felt. Sometimes it's like a bridge that could either bring you across or leave you stranded and sadly, today around the world it seems like the majority of students have their attitudes formed at the wrong places and at the wrong time. What do I mean? Let me explain. Many think that because they come from a prestigious school or did well in school, or maybe mentally they think that they are smarter because of the education route they choose – which is a shallow thought to begin with, that they come off as nothing much but cocky, arrogant and with much pride. But, yes, I have to admit that these are general statements with a few exceptionally good kids from top schools; however there are many truths to it. One of them is that your grades in school do not equate to how well you will flourish in life; even if they are good, it may increase the chances of a higher-paying job, but it does not guarantee it. Another – it does not equate to you being able to work well with your peers on a daily basis. And another – it does not equate to you being smarter when it really counts; on paper you may be an A+ student, but in reality you might lack the much needed common sense to even do the simplest thing like asking for clarifications to quicken your work process. And I'd like to reiterate – common sense is very rare these days.

The rapid change in the working world has many bosses going for the right attitude first, then knowledge and skills behind. And my friend, though attitude is a word; just like all other theories and formulas, it takes a lot of effort to work on it. Especially having a positive attitude; having one not only makes you attractive, it opens the doors to many other things like better communication. But if you're on the other side and stuck up I've got some insight news for you, and the headlines read, "Google rejects top student with eleven As' because of poor attitude." So, on one hand, you have all your check boxes for great results and knowledge ticked, whereas because of one simple thing – your attitude—you flunked one of the biggest opportunities of your life. The moral of the story? Be careful how you carry yourself, your attitude in particular; no one owes you anything, and, if you're not careful, you'll blow up everything. And do not just think that your good attitude is to be just kept within your work place, because not only will word spread around that you have a stinking attitude, but more importantly it has become your natural state. You're very likely to do it to everyone you meet. Imagine meeting someone along the street, and unknowingly you laugh at a boy who has dyslexia for being slow. You walk across the room bragging at your quick learning abilities, ignoring his crushed feelings and you further mock at the boy's parents for having such a child. Days later you go for an interview, and it is for your dream job at a huge MNC and you realize that the interviewer, your future boss, is the boy's father. Guess what? You've lost the job even before the interview begins.

Speaking of Google, currently Google no longer hires base on the academic GPA of a student but rather how fast they can think on their feet. They are looking out for people who, despite having the probability of messing around would chance upon a new solution as to the guy who plays with the same formula all the time despite producing results.

Today, the world has more people with higher levels of education, and certainly the standard will continue to rise with every generation. But the truth, the ugly and sad truth is this, with every passing generation there seems to be an increasing number of world problems appearing; more wars, more plagues and now it seems like the only certainty is uncertainty and these weren't the scenarios decades ago. Yes, there were world crises even at the beginning of time and there were uncertainties but education has not done its part on the larger field. Yes education has brought us great things; globalization, better healthcare and standard of living but to me – it failed at the exact place where it was supposed to be most effective – it failed to bring about a world with better attitudes, instead it brought a world of selfishness. Education has taught more people to be more inward looking, more self-centered and has certainly brought a greater depression than the Great depression in the 1930s. We have more money, but we sure have many more problems than money can solve. We have more brains but our brains have fewer solutions to life. Education may not be the key to solve everything as more problems are arising even as the education ladder grows.

Here are my reasons for the above. Growing up in a neighborhood school, I could really feel that it was more of a family school; people were more caring, even though there were competitions to get better grades, it was rarely personal. Whereas in top schools, it's common to hear people backstabbing each other or even teaching each other the wrong things on purpose so as to get ahead, and because they have grown up with such conducts and beliefs, it is only normal for them to carry forth all that they've acquired over time. For sure you would say that I am biased, but the facts remain. Though there are different types of students in all schools, but the students that fall within the "good grades but poor attitude" outnumber the "sub-par grades but great attitude" easily. Stinking pride goes everywhere, sadly, sometimes it's not a choice but rather it's in-built. Pride is a kind of attitude, too. Yes, I know the phrase, "My character is fixed, but my attitude towards you depends on how you treat me." But honestly, it's like the old dude who sits in the rocking chair, claiming that everything stinks until he realizes that actually, it was the faeces on his nose that stunk.

Don't blame kids if parents don't show them the Way of life. We are all in a mess and depressed because we hold on too tightly on a piece of paper that dissolves in water and too loosely on people who endure hardship - all in the name of "save face" and money. The younger generation should be taught about hard work and the value of each individual, not respect based on the job. Are we then to disrespect toilet cleaners and hawker workers because we say "these people have tough laborious jobs because they did not study hard." However, knowing that hawkers come from all sorts of backgrounds and even include degree holders and illiterate workers but they both have the same thing in common – passion. Now you wouldn't be saying that if you were in their shoes or you know of people working in hawkers. I bet you'll think twice about disrespecting such "prestigious" jobs if they were your parents or grandparents.

With that said, I still believe that there are people out there with brains, and character. People, who are cool, calm and fun, I tip my hat off to you, and I'm proud to say that not all hope is lost because of such people.

Things will never change let alone go back to where they came from. That's why my belief is that I am for learning just not education. Learning is for life, and education is for the first few years or maybe decades of your life. Education and learning may seem to be related but they're not. Education is what you pay for, get graded for and at the end you can get certified for something; some even buy their certificates. Education is kept strictly within a school compound. Education forces kids to swallow everything in their textbooks and then come exam time, they just vomit out everything. And everyone goes on without developing their brains for proper use, such as the understanding of things. Learning may be part of education but surely learning goes on even after you've graduated. Learning is up to an individual, it has no fixed modules or topics. Learning is based on curiosity; learning teaches you how to adapt to changes, learning is knowledge gained through experience. Sometimes I feel that one of the best and quickest way to learn is not through the textbook but through talking with people who have valuable experience and knowledge in the topic on hand; reading the textbook may take you two weeks, reading with understanding may take you one month. But by talking to people who know more than the textbook and more than what you are taught in school through their own experience for a quick ten minutes, could give you more than the main point of the textbook and also extra tips not found in a textbook, of which you may never even know of just by reading. But still it all begins with your attitude towards them, and how you communicate. If you come off as having a "know it all" aura, than you will never get a single thing from them. But if you come off as respectful and curious, certainly you'll leave with more than what you can handle.

Education is: going through the problems than taking a fixed test at the end. You have a fixed system in place to grade you, there will always be someone there to guide and to push you and regardless of what you do, you still get a grade. It's like being in a box; no matter what you do you're confined within it. Learning is: going through the tests first before you solve the problems. There are no grades, no one to push you but just you alone. There are no ceilings, and this makes it a little bit more challenging because no one will point out your mistakes like how a teacher does. Which do you think is more realistic in a real world?

Education has allowed more people to grow smarter in a shorter time, but it has also created a wall of knowledge that has the vertical height greatly outgrowing the horizontal length of understanding things. For example, someone can be greatly educated, great with results but poor in basic daily communications. I think it is also safe to say that many students are stuck in "bookepedia." They think that all answers can be found inside their textbooks. Life answers, and answers to solving your work issues. Let's face it, the chances are slim even when you work because it's usually a sudden "discovery" or how well or quick you can think on your feet for solutions. News flash, whatever that you're studying is likely to be outdated because your predecessors needed time to create your textbooks; roughly five years. On top of it, you add on the ever-changing environment; something way faster than your computers' processor and you're back to square one. Your knowledge will never be up to date, simply because the internet has outdone everyone when it comes to giving the latest and most accurate updates. It seems like the one who gathered much did not have too much, and the one who gathered little did not have too little. Certainly such truths will never be found inside a textbook.

Still I hope people do not derive their characters or how they treat others based on their results. One too many kids these days grow up being overly confident just because they do well in school, they think that it is a huge deal, no doubt it's a great achievement, and however have you noticed that these achievements are only found within your "four walls"? This is why exposure to different things in life; things not related to paper results can prevent them from growing up with a narcissistic mind-set solely caused by placing too high of an emphasis on education and the results.

ARE YOU HAPPY?

Let's face it, there are only countless doctors and lawyers and scientists out there, and how many of us will actually be one? If you have a dream go for it. I am not knocking you off, because I believe that one should work towards a dream. Still, I know many people upon getting their "dream" job end up being unhappy because they are stuck.

These formulas we learn in school can only be used in a certain environment, and cannot be used most of the time unless you are in the field of one of the above mentioned jobs. That's why I think a soft skill – a personal relationship skill is the most vital skill and can be used almost everywhere, in and out of the classroom and office.

Whatever you do, I hope you are happy, I hope you do not study for the sake of stopping your parents from nagging at you. I know of cases whereby parents force their will upon their children and other people's children, of which is totally wrong. And mind you these kids are growing and are mature-thinking young adults at the ages of 17 to 20. You may think you know more than they, but you may be surprised that times have changed and what you perceive to know or believe might not be the key to life or even happiness as it was during your yester-years.

REAL LIFE LEARNING
NOT FOUND IN TEXTBOOKS

Once while buying a drink, I started a random conversation with the cashier and this was how it went.

Me: This is your part-time job while studying?

Cashier: well, I failed two subjects during my O levels, and I have to re-take them again next year. (With a little sigh and I could sense condemnation within her)

Me: no worries, at least you're the rare few who understand that life is not based on your school results and don't feel bad because you've failed once. You've still got another chance; all you need is to pace yourself. Don't burn yourself out from over-studying before your exams. Your openness and honesty is something you can never get out of your O-level grades.

(Now it was obvious that she had blushed from my comments)

Cashier: (With much excitement) well finally someone's talking sense! All my friends are saying the total opposite and making a huge deal out of O-levels.

This is what I call realistic learning about life outside of the classroom; something education would never be able to produce, if so almost non-existent. It was not out of paper qualifications that I respected her, but rather the way she presented herself, without airy pride that made the difference. The key was not to remind her about her failures but to let her know that life is much more than a piece of paper that dissolves when it touches water. Now I'm not saying that it's okay to not study when you have to but just through a simple conversation you could easily tell that she had a renewed perspective about life, and I certainly believe that she would pass her exams this time.

This is what we call real learning. It seems like people who are open to understand and not just believe that grades are everything seem to be more open, honest and realistic about life!

The majority of the people have become keyboard warriors; good at saying things behind the screen because they either have no guts or cannot communicate face to face. And it doesn't help that we have moved into an IT age, whereby almost everything related to life and learning is done through the computer and the internet. I find it awkwardly amazing that even though one may live in a well-developed country with a good education, for example, Singapore, many people, especially the younger generations, lack the skills to communicate with their peers, colleagues, bosses, or strangers, let alone getting their ideas across to the other party. But I do marvel that it has some really great positive side effects, namely, the saving of the earth because lesser trees are being cut down to produce notes and work sheets.

However, the greatest irony of all, with regards to the IT issue of kids and parents being glued to their devices, of which is also the number one factor that kills real bonding time, is that even IT greats such as Steve Jobs and Bill Gates had no such problems! How is it possible for the creator to almost eradicate the negative side effects on their own while others are dying to it? It's simple, because they never started at all! Another puzzling thing to me is: how is it possible for a drop out like Steve jobs to have simple dining etiquette while people who spend more time with a relatively higher level of education not have the etiquette of simply not using your phone over meals? Not just so that you can give proper attention to those around you, but actually have proper communication whereby everyone is either listening or talking? I'll tell you what both Mr Jobs and Mr Gates did, and it's a real no brainer. They demonstrated to their kids first, by not showing up at the dining table without their phones; of which their kids followed through. Then they talked to their kids about life, discussed geography, history and their day. (Oh wait I forgot to tell you, they run companies worth billions, and if they can get away from their phones for an hour or so, I'm very sure even if you're a millionaire you could do it too).

Research shows that, apart from killing bonding time, spending too much time using your mobile devices and other electronic devices could be an eventual silent killer. In just a year the amount of average stress on the cervical spine amounts to 700 to 1400 hours, and could add up to 60 pounds of pressure. In the long run, this position; hunched-forward increases the risk of spinal wear and tear. Now that is a problem that people with smaller heads have to also deal with, so if you've got a big head, you're in company![1]

STUDYING? OR JUST FOR THE SAKE OF STUDYING?

As mentioned above, I believe that studying is good, but when you come to a crossroad to choose between further studying by paying on your own and knowing that you might be stuck in debt for a long time and choosing not to further study, the latter is the better choice.

A man told me in the face "Students from polytechnics are those who can't study while JC students are those who can study and have brighter futures." I'd like to see how he and not his kids fare when he realize that it's not about the qualification or certificate but the person's character. Sadly I didn't give him Kieroy style words whooping about how many people with stacks of certificates being jobless. I can't be bothered to revive the walking dead. At the end it's about being at the right place and time and having the right perspective, and certainly not where you come from.

In my opinion, if you are out to just get a degree and be done with, but at the back of your mind you have the weight of the debts tied with it – don't do it. I know people will say that this is short-sightedness, and a huge sense of ignorance. I also know that because in an economic cycle, things will not be perpetually stuck at the recession phase and that a degree will give you a higher leverage as to your peers with lower education. However, you often only hear of the higher paying jobs and almost never hear about the debt situation that the student goes into, and it's a very long-term debt,

---

[1]   http://time.com/3595976/spine-phone/

and a lifelong issue. Secondly, having more money gets you more stuff, but the real question here is—are you really happy? So many people close the doors on other opportunities in life. Things that come only once in a life time, such as their dream jobs of which are not even closely related to what you study, but because you choose to study only for the sake of doing it, you missed that one chance. And by no means am I referring to the few rare dropouts who make it big. Thirdly, a higher pay means you may get to pay off your debt quicker as you progress up the corporate ladder right? Wrong! Many graduates are not willing to take up low level jobs with lower remunerations, therefore prolonging the process of paying off their debts. On top of it, many have a shopaholic attitude, therefore they spend money that they have yet to earn or do not have or think that they may have, you see it's easy to get stuck in debt through online shopping. All because we only see the physical goods and not our money physically, and because we do not see our money physically we actually do not really know how much we are actually spending.

As I've said above – these days the only certainty is uncertainty. There are countless people in the USA with a bachelor's degree who are jobless (In 2011, out of 1.5 million, 53.6% under the age of 25 are jobless. Figures may change – good or bad but you get the whole idea)[2] or doing an odd job that not only is the job unrelated to the degree but also these jobs can be done even without a degree, many college graduates were heavily represented in jobs that require a high school diploma or less for example, being a barista, or a cashier or even working in McDonald's. And despite all these you could still find happiness and satisfaction in life. Though the figures are from the USA, and you may be reading this in Singapore, there's a reason why people say "when America sneezes Singapore gets the cold."

---

[2] http://www.thewire.com/business/2012/04/536-young-graduates-dont-have-jobs/51459/

Burst in education bubble.

These are my personal views on the current education system, though I may not have data, or rather, since it is near impossible to find an accurate data because the general news on school and education is more often keen to show how good they are statistically than to show the bigger picture of the current market situation of the world's economy which has way more higher certificate holders than jobs available for such people. I think that the education bubble has long burst, and that people are still blindly going into getting a piece of certificate that they do not like but rather just for getting themselves back into school. But I think it could be a better opportunity for an individual to go out to the workplace first and then re-consider their options after. Especially if you're an aspiring entrepreneur, the couple of years in school and the debt can be used to fund your career. Yes, it's a high-risk move, but at least you gave your best and made a choice that you could say you've regretted less as to going to school. No one really knows the answers, (honestly no one knows the answers to life as well, no matter how smart they sound, not even me, I know nuts, I just know my opinions that's all) however I also think that the things with regards to "education is extremely important and that the ceiling is only going to increase" may no longer hold true despite the signs of it showing likewise. I believe that the world will eventually return to a point, such as our parent's era of those in the 1960s whereby education is not the main factor that helped people grow but rather it was more on the personal mind-set and understanding of things that made things grow, because now uncertainty has become more than ever the new certainty. Back then, people were lowly educated, but yet even today it seems like they still know more things than those who eat their textbooks for breakfast, lunch and dinner.

I may be wrong, this is just what I see happening sooner than later, just that everything seems to be going against all that I have said here.

My point here is – do not think too much of a degree or further studying because the main key about life is not a one-way train but to just keep having a wider perspective about things, should you find a faculty or course that you know helps you sharpen your skills in pursuing what you want in life, and love doing by all means go ahead. You are a human, not a robot; this is your life, not someone else's life. Live your own life and be happy!

ARE YOU THE TEACHER WHO ONLY TEACHES BUT NEVER LEARNS THE TRUTH OF TEACHING?

I have something to say about teachers, they are great and without them many students will not be what they are today. However, things have greatly changed, I almost cannot believe that most teachers today are more concerned about climbing up the corporate leader as to really caring for and teaching students on how to be better persons and making the world a better place. So many teachers today have lost it, they are only concerned about making themselves look good on paper, and, for example, all they care about is the results produced by the students and not how they grow up individually. Of course, you'll say it's impossible because of the number of students in a class, but how hard is it to reach out to a few students first, and then allowing these few to pass on the flame to their classmates? Is not holistic learning about aiding the student to find their purpose in life and also to contribute back towards the society? Then why make things look as though it's all about the grades? I am very thankful to have teachers who cared for my growth as an individual as well as a student who takes the exam papers, without them it's hard to imagine life the way it is today. Teaching is a selfless art; it's all about giving back to the kids, and then empowering these kids to make the world a better place. That is the main role of an educator, not some teacher who comes in and grinds the class just for good grades. If you are a teacher with such philosophy, I hope you reconsider it because it's not your life that is at stake but the kids that are the future. Equip them with the skill today and watch them flourish tomorrow.

DO YOU DEBATE OR ARE YOU IN BATE?

Firstly, bate is defined as "an angry mood" by Oxford Dictionaries. And growing up in an Asian classroom and hearing stories of the western classrooms I cannot help but think that most Asian students are actually in bate instead of doing a debate. The westerners are more open towards debate and can keep their cool whereas Asians get into all sorts of personal attacks and ruin the meaning of debate; a discussion.

I believe it is in the exposure of the students. Westerners are less conservative and more open towards talking to strangers and therefore have a natural gab when it comes to discussing things even in class, whereas most Asians are rather conservative and therefore would be taken aback when someone of a different culture gets their idea across in a more direct manner.

MORAL

The thing about every individual is that we all have a certain standard of morality; it is based on our personal gut feeling. Many times in life, prior to your actions and through your decision-making you've probably thought, does it feel right? What will the outcome of my actions be? Individually, we all have a set of ideas or values that aid us in guiding our daily actions and to a certain extent it is governed by our thoughts and beliefs; what and how we are brought up in life. And certainly there is no fixed way nor is there a way that is 100% correct, because just like life, there are no grades, but only the tests and through the test of life you'll get to know whether your morals are right or wrong through your feelings at the end. Did it feel good in the long run? Or was it just a moment of soul satisfying and hell guilty after?

Everyone would love to sparkle and shine, with good actions, thoughts and words linked to his name and reputation, however the catch is this – not everything that looks like a diamond is a real diamond. It may look like one, but the dimensions and quality can never be the same. With just a few "knocks" and then you'll see some cracks on your fake diamonds. Probably that's the reason why man made diamonds come cheaper. Just so everyone could afford it, to flash it and to let it bling but more importantly to differentiate the real goods from the fake goods. A real diamond can be easily differentiated from a man-made diamond; simply by using some heat. By first heating the diamond for 30 seconds, and then dipping it immediately into ice cold water. The result of the quick expansion and contraction will easily overwhelm the tensile strength of the weaker stone and cause it to shatter from the inside. Real diamonds are strong and sturdy and will not break away under such environments. Or simply put both stones on a piece of newspaper article, the one that can be seen through is fake; because a real diamond is able to cause refractions so sharp that it is hard to see the text behind it. In the same way, people with low moral values or lack moral values can be seen through easily.

With all these said, the point is not that humans do not, will not, and cannot make mistakes, but the root is that on a daily basis, or in the long run what does the individual keep? Does he do the majority of things morally correct that resound not just internally but to those around him who also agrees with him or does he lack the consistency, so much so that even when he does good things often people still question his motives? It's like a weighing scale, you're wise enough to judge. Just remember, if one comes cheap, the cheaper he'll go than before he came.

CONNECTION, A TWO WAY LINE

Without connection, nothing happens. Sounds cliché right? Certainly, but you seldom hear about attracting connections. You'd probably hear "building your connections through networking" a thousand times throughout your lifetime, though it is right and one of the fastest ways to expand. I'd like to add in another gear to your drive. But first, connections always start with yourself and that is why the impressions that you leave can either be a future stairway to heaven or a nightmare awaiting for you.

IS FIRST IMPRESSION THAT IMPORTANT?

Yes, to a great extent. After all, memories are why things keep on going, either for good or for bad. (Especially for ladies since it has been proven that ladies have better memories and that is why they often bring up the past). It's like how you build a house of bricks, if the foundations are solid and strong then only will the top be stable when the strong winds blow. And it is not just the ladies, but it is almost impossible to erase a bad lasting image, imagine coming in to work and showing that you have a poor attitude; you're lazy and are sharp tongued. That alone has already irritated a few people and then you add on the bad news that spreads about you, before you know it, the whole world is against you. Still if that is you, do not lose hope. (Of course the easiest way out is to quit, jump ship into another organisation, and hopefully you are able to turn over a new leaf; but trust me, it's extremely difficult, because once it's part of your trait it's likely to be there for a long time. And even though science has done wonders from erasing bad memories on rats, it is nowhere near using the technology on humans. So forget the idea of throwing countless people into the lab and have their bad memories of you erased) But what you can do is to start afresh mentally first, it's going to be hard because people will be very sceptical especially on your first few tries, but you've got to keep grinding your way through. It may not be perfect like before but it would certainly improve. The key is to distance yourself from the people you've caused friction with first then showing up only for doing good deeds. However, I've to warn you if you've tried and it still doesn't work, don't lose your life over it, pick yourself up, learn from it and move on.

However it might seem weird at times like there's a role-swap; those who may be well-liked at first seem to be disliked much later on and then the opposite; those who are disliked much at first may seem to be really well liked later on. Should you be the latter, keep doing your part and the fruits will appear before you even know it. Sometimes humans are attracted to things that are "fresh," and often times the reason for it is because they think it's something refreshing, when in fact it's like eating an expired chocolate cake when you're in desperate need for some sugar-rush and then paying the price of getting diarrhea later on. Picture this: two 18-year-old male teenagers, one who is 6 feet tall and average looking while the other is 5 feet 4 inches with a boyish look. On the first appearance, the majority of the people will zoom right in to talk to the smaller guy and pay almost zero attention to the other guy only because the smaller guy looks more attractive at the moment. Unknowingly, the smaller guy is lazy, rude, and has an "I can do no wrong" personality and the bigger guy has a better working attitude and a cheerful smile and a down-to-earth personality. Who do you think has a better ending? When the tables turn it's obvious that sometimes people end up questioning themselves "Why did I bother to know the cocky dude better? I should have just spent more time having a good laugh with Frankenstein instead!" That's why never judge a man by virtue of his looks or height.

Attracting Connections

The point that I'd like to bring across with attracting connections is that most of the responsibility falls on you. Let me explain, things first start with you showing up physically. Honestly, if you do not show up, no one will believe you. Then maybe you could be doing something well, or maybe you are well known for having such a great set of skills or maybe you possess an attractive characteristic or personality that makes people drawn to you. At the same time, because you are skilled, being confident is the fruit that bears off by itself. And confidence is contagious, it spreads around, confidence attracts many people; people who have low self-esteem or maybe even depression or a lack of direction in life. Whatever that has any life of uncertainty is drawn to that piece of certainty and it will give you an unexpected boost that not many individuals regardless of age or working experience will have. There is a great emphasis in carrying yourself well; though you may think that as you walk forward no one will trace your foot-steps, but you're wrong. If you've ever walked on snow, you'd realize that with every step you take on the path, you leave behind a trace of your footsteps for others to not only follow you but to also track you down. And carrying yourself well starts off even without you knowing it – in your daily communications with others you may think that it is only between two humans, however people can see, read and understand your body language from afar and they can easily decipher it or make up something inside their heads and then it will spread.

In the past I'd often hear about how you have to be savvy with your hands or rather have a "know-how" skill, without a doubt it's great to have hands-on skills, as you can tell from above I took some time to elaborate on the importance and different type of skills sets. With know how you see things with a certain dimension. But today, things have changed a little, many today are saying of "who you know." Not that the "know-how" phase has died but today, knowing someone powerful could turn your misery into a miracle. With know-who, you see things from another dimension. Now imagine joining the two known siblings – you'd certainly get to see things from different dimensions.

THE STORY OF THE KNOW BROTHERS.

I once heard a story of a powerful banker who was the president of a large city bank. He was standing in front of the automatic teller one day while it performed a transaction rather slowly, which was unusual. After some time, he was heard saying "COME ON, IT'S ME!" Being the president of the bank doesn't give you special connections with the ATM. The moral of the story? Sometimes it's not about your official position, because once you leave that post you're no longer the same especially if you get fired along the way. Do not make a big commotion about your position, because real respect and connections comes without a post in the office. It's better if your connections come from outside in, as to, in from the outside. Sometimes in life you need more than just "know-how" or "know-who." Other times it's about from the ground to the top. If you get along well with people on the ground, it's only a matter of time before people from the top notice you. It's only a matter of time before good things about you spread to the top management.

But, of course, with every sibling, having some sibling rivalry and friendly fights are normal, but yet it's like a tug of war, no one wants to give in or even lose, both make the claim that one is more important than the other with neither realizing the importance of unity and the strength of bonding. That is until the most important person - their father "who knows you" shows up. With it comes the last dimension that completes the whole structure. Needless to say, that without their father, neither son would be present. The key is this – I've learned that in life, especially when it comes to connections, it's like having a domino effect, if you place your dominos at the right place and start at the right place, everything will fall in line. It's the same for good and bad connections. On the positive side, if people know you for bringing in positive attributes things are likely to go in your favor but on the flip side if you are known to bring in negative attributes then things are more than likely to work against you. Knowing how or knowing who is like toppling the dominos either from the mid-way point or maybe even a third of the whole domino set; though you will cause dominos to fall, it doesn't bring in the full effect of the picture. However, if people knew you, that is to say "who knows you," it's like toppling the dominos from the first piece and then eventually you get a nicer picture because the dominos do not fall against each other.

If there is anything I can share from my personal experience here, is that I've a knack for attracting people and connections. This means all I have to do is to just show up physically. (Yes it sounds extremely arrogant and prideful, filled with great hubris I know. And I do not apologize for it. It's fair to say that I also get unwanted attention at times, too.) By the same token, I am also a walking target for many, either good or bad. People just enjoy rubbing off me, the good ones enjoy my company, and the bad ones just try their best to get under my skin to irritate me. Maybe it's my personality, maybe it's the way I carry myself or the way I talk or maybe I'm just favored. Along the way, I've come to realize that most of the time I seem to not only get along better with my superiors compared to many of my peers but they seem to also favor me much more than my peers, and that could be the reason why I'm hated, too. Maybe it's their jealousy? I do not know, but this I know—God has blessed me like a magnet to attract good things for my life and I'm sure attracting connections is one. (Thank God!)

This method of either knowing who or who knows you work great but it has a limit to it. Certainly it is one of the smartest ways to get around things, especially when you're in a dire situation however things do not just stop at one point. Whenever it comes to working, hard work takes pre-eminence over the former things; know-how, know-who and who knows you. These three can certainly get you to places whereby hard work alone may never get you there, but once you're there it all goes back to grinding another brick wall. Working smart is the ideal situation, but as we all know, in life there really isn't an "ideal situation," that's why in science you often hear scientist say "in an ideal situation.....this would work," because they know in the real world it's near impossible.

I will not discuss financial investment and its methods because the main chunk is about work ethic not money making moves.

LOYALTY

Loyalty should not be a word without meaning; it takes two hands to clap. I wish people could learn something from our former generations; whereby even when times get tough they do not quit on each other nor do they talk about getting other people involve. It should not come to a point of comparing what the other person or company can do or bring but to work together on whatever difficulties both are facing.

If your boss lets you go or ill treats you it just means that they are cheap and dull. There will always be people who are smarter, more talented and someone to take your place but countless people overlook the impact of one person; someone important and influential that can make great cultural differences within the organisation. But you can also tell yourself that it is their loss, because whatever you have or can bring is uniquely yours, you may not be the smartest guy or quickest learner, but for one simple reason; because you can influence the decisions of your peers at work it would make a whole lot of difference for the organisation just to have you. But wait, I know you're thinking, "Who do you think you are?" Honestly, no persons really believe in themselves, that's why you get employees who are like dead trees waiting to collapse. There's no empowerment, and therefore you see most people just dragging their feet to work because they are not willing to be the change person or the person that brings sparks to light up the room.

EFFICIENCY

There is a reason why meetings are usually long without any solid findings or actions, but rather it's often to be like a bunch of people going around the same molehill. It would certainly do everyone good if they'd just attack the problems, discuss the key points to solving the problem and then carrying out the needed actions. But sadly it doesn't happen because there are too many mouths and too little brains at work. More like NATO – No action, talk only.

Being efficient is a choice, it is better to spend some time to plan your next actions then to waste a whole lot of time beating around the bush. With that said, it'll be great if people of the same like-minded actions come together, with only one voice with the rest hearing, and to only interrupt when they have a better idea. Of course such like-minded people must not have the same mind-set of skiving or pushing work away all the time. Learning to say "no" to some jobs given to you will help you get further; it is one thing to decline every secondary job that is only hindering your primary job, and another to decline everything just because you dislike it. You may dislike it, but just like fertilizer, it's the primary source of growth for plants.

On a personal level, it would be a quick basket if people will just do whatever they need to do instead of thinking about the cons more often than the thought of "just do it." I think efficiency also starts with having a clear expectation and defined goals of what is needed of each individual, this means knowing what one's job scope is and when it is expected to be completed.

DURABILITY

Durability comes with health. If you have no health, you won't even have work ethic. It is the simple things, such as your own healthcare that makes a whole lot of difference. I know of countless people who only visit the dentist for scaling and polishing when they have a toothache caused by a build-up of bacteria in their mouth and gums. Whereby such should be done at least once every six months, we all have busy schedule, but I think it's a wiser move to save yourself from severe tooth aches and more money incurred caused by postponing the important things.

It is like fitness at work; just as it takes time to build up your stamina for a run, so does it take time for you to have a high level of endurance at work. Being durable is all about conditioning both your physical wellbeing as well as mental and emotional wellbeing. Mentally you just have to grind things out, emotionally, learn to de-baggage all your useless baggage.

Taking care of yourself is a key attribute to being successful as well, simply because there is no one other than yourself to reach your goal or dreams.

POSITIVE STUMBLING?

Sometimes I do wonder if I grew up way too fast; before my time. But at the same time I find it relatively easy to connect with people older than myself. I'd like to think that it is a compliment that I have had parents asking me about how to encourage their kids to go to work and to stop them from being lazy (I hope by reading this book it would help).

I guess it could be said of as a positive stumbling for me as I find it a challenge to blend in with the majority of my peers, because going through the different things in life has made me see things in different perspectives, partly, I believe, it is because I have gone through things way before them. And it is because of such, at times not only do I find it a challenge communicating with my peers but also blending in. Yet when it comes to communicating with the older generations it is much easier. These things are my own personal experience, though it was initially tough and growing through life by not having a childhood that is common amongst my peers, or even my generations and those to come. Not to say that I had a bad childhood, probably just a different experience.

In return, however, I got things and ideas that could not be found through playing with toys and gadgets or even getting things easily. It was a huge trade-off considering the fact that you only live life at a tender age once, the age where people are playing way more than working. It also didn't help with friends constantly saying things like, "you're wasting your time working" or, "Why work so hard?" or, "Why not just ask for allowances from your parents?" What's worse is that even the adults are saying the same thing to me such as "Why work? Your parents have money." But I've always ignored them, so much so that I think the reason why I'm able to unconsciously impress the older generation is because I just do the things that I need to do; without caring so much about people's opinion of how I should be like at a certain age or point in my life. With these said, I'm also sure that there are many people out there that share the same thoughts as me; and may even know more than me, but I just had the passion to write things down. And honestly, the only thing to remind me to keep going is to look-over my shoulder and realize that there are countless people having tougher, poorer lives than I do.

THE "IT" FACTOR

It's just unexplainable. It's like one of those superstar move that only a few people can pull off. It's like having people like you just for who you are, to a point whereby you just know that once you open your mouth to let your request fly out, it's almost like you know it would be a "yes" before it happens. It's like a preferential treatment that only you get. I guess it boils down to a mixture of communication, soft skills, some charisma and much favor. I would think work ethic contributes greatly to this "it" factor, because at some point you need to show the goods when all talk is done. I'm very blessed to have "it" going constantly on a roll for me almost everywhere I go even outside of work even when I meet strangers. I thank God for it.

Personal working experience from age 14 to 21

The following are jobs that I have done previously during my school holidays as well as a full time student, and the duration could be as short as a few days to a few months, not that I am a job hopper but rather because each event or contract had a certain timeframe. Going through the different jobs helped to shape my mind about work and life therefore the result is this book. Of which is based on my personal thoughts, experience and opinions. As for my perspective on money, I learned about it the hard way as I stopped taking allowances ever since I was 18. The way I earned it made me realize that money does not come easily, but also money is meant to not only improve one's standard of living but to also help others. For me I usually do it by giving – such as buying someone else a meal.

The following are not in chronological order. They are according to job scopes.

Selling and packing books in my school bookshop.

This was my very first job, and I only worked because I wanted to earn some money apart from gaining experience as well as to pass some time during the school holidays. I was 14 years old; looking back now the pay was pathetic by all standards in Singapore. I got paid only $3.50 per hour. The job required me to attend to customers and unpack books from the delivery pallets and arrange them inside the bookstore, it was dusty and boring, but it kick-started my confidence in talking to people. Time passed slowly, but that was when I learned that sometimes work is tough because you're just waiting to pass time. But I felt good getting my first pay check of which came in to be about only $21 a day after working 6 hours. It was also then that I learned the true value of money, because, after deducting my food and transport cost, I was only left with $12 to bring home.

DISTRIBUTION OF FLYERS

Back then I was 14, and working with friends was the cool thing. We couldn't care less about doing a proper job, so while the four of us were split into groups of two, my friend and I were tasked to be stationed outside an office building. Lo and behold, we went up to the office toilet, dumped three quarters of our flyers into the rubbish bin and just sat around wasting time. After some time, we met up with the other two at a secluded staircase and we ended up playing cards! (Okay, I know you're thinking "a bunch or rascals, killing more trees and wasting people's money." Everyone's got to grow up, and that is why I'm writing to tell people not to make the same mistakes as I did). Years later when I was 17, I landed the same job but for a different company and this time I had grown up. My friend and I were tasked to stand under the hot sun from 11 a.m. to 2 p.m. just to distribute the flyers to the office crowd during lunch to promote a new shop at Boat Quay. Not only were we two perspiring as though we just came out from the showers, I had to wear a large signage across my front and back, and it made things worse because the phrase "good things come in small sizes" just seemed like a huge lie. I had issues walking around because these boards were going past my knee caps and it made it very hard to walk, every step I took, I had a mini obstacle to clear and the probability of me tripping was there.

WAREHOUSE PACKER

This was my second job dealing with cardboards and plastic wrappers on a regular basis. My part was to retrieve and set up the cardboard boxes before shoving in the products and then wrapping them up with a plastic wrapper. It was a manual job, and it was here that I heard an older worker tell me, "Come on, you don't have to be gentle with the boxes, it's a box not a girl." From then on, I realized that I needed to get more assertive and aggressive towards these boxes. The foreman or floor leader was strict, she kept hurrying us to complete more packaging, and from there I realized that maybe it's because these people were lowly-educated and, therefore, they had poor management skills as well as PR skills. Maybe I am wrong, you know as a 15 year old, you'd think that if people are hard on you at work there're likely to have come from a poor background, but growing up now I realize that these individuals had responsibilities to fulfil else they might lose their jobs. Still, I disagree on how things were done, for example tracking your movements as though you were a criminal and even during your rest periods you felt like you were being watched over all the time. From then on I realized that I really wasn't good with hands-on stuff, nor was I really keen to do such jobs. With this job, my parents initially told me not to take it up, not only because the pay was low, but also because of the tough working environment. They persuaded me not to do it; we had a rift over it, because I told them, I gave my word to the manager—who was my relative—that I'd do the job, and although it was easy to pull out of it, I pressed on because I had my pride and dignity.

WORKING AT A HAWKER

The one thing I'd like to tell everyone is, whether you frequent the hawker or not– respect these people because it is an extremely tough job, not just standing for hours but standing directly in front of the heat. And also hawkers do not have an easy life, some get up as early as 4:30 a.m. just to prepare their ingredients, but the main consequence is that in the long run these people pay a higher price of having lung-related diseases because of the smoke that enters their lungs. Though I just tried out my hands at serving food, it was really at that time whereby I had to be stable in juggling the utensils and foods on the tray as well as having a quick mental calculation for the change required. Trust me, it isn't fun when the orders keep piling up and the hawker is so crowded and humid. These days, I know that there are many kids even as young as 11 helping out at their parents' stall, and whenever I see them I really tip my hat off to them because they're really experiencing life outside their comfort zone instead of staying home just to watch some dramas.

WASHING CARS

A relative runs his own used-car dealership in Singapore, so when I was 15 I decided to follow him to work. I ended up washing cars ever since then, all the way until now, whenever it was needed. Not that we couldn't afford to hire car washers, back then money was really good, and I had a choice not to do it, but I just wanted to do it. It wasn't an easy job, because apparently on average I washed eight cars a day. The majority of them would be continental cars of the likes of BMW and Mercedes-Benz which were larger than the average Japanese cars, and every day I'd wash the cars again because the very next day these cars would get dirty as a result of the dust from the roads, or worse, because of the dry stain caused by the rain. I'd sweat more than I could ever imagine – the moment I reached the office, I'd go in, put my belongings aside, and go straight into washing cars. It didn't help that the water hose had moss all over it and I ended up having moss inside my fingertips too, and this made my hand itch daily. I worked for free and rejected any money given by him.

GLOBAL DRINK COMPANY

This job taught me to eat dust. It was during one of the festive period that I did this job and I'd work nine hours daily, and despite being sold the idea of, "oh, don't worry, these sells out on its own. All you have to do is just simple customer service, and replenish *some stocks* when it runs out," looking back now I still think that one should greatly consider the words of a female supervisor, I now think I was really gullible back then! But anyway, I took the job, every day I would transfer about six pallets of drinks, some were in cartons of 30 cans, some were in a pack of 12 bottles of 1.5 litres each, some were tetra packs, some were boxes of 6 cans from the loading bay into the shop (in my mind I was wondering to myself all the time "which part of some stocks look like 6 pallets of drinks?) And from the shop onto the sheltered tents where all the other drink companies had displayed their products for sale. I spent the bulk of my time carrying drinks and I seldom attended to any customers because the drinks got sold out so fast, I was desperately refilling the stocks. And, yes, the drinks weren't light, despite having a mini pusher, it didn't aid me much, in fact it got me more frustrated because the wheels kept falling off!

However, I did have quite an adventure working as well. On a few occasions, the drinks that were stacked up to 1.2m crashed towards the ground! One time I didn't know better because even though I knew that the grounds were slightly uneven I never dreamt that something small would cause such a huge chaos. I had bottles popping up and drinks splashing all over as a result of the carbonated gas and the impact that it had when it hit the ground. In total I think it was an estimated 240 large bottles that I had to clear, when that happened I really thought of quitting because it was already draining physically to carry so many drinks daily let alone deal with all the sticky drinks and plastic wrappers. Another time the same thing happened again, but on a smaller scale. As I was turning my back, and, as a result of the aisle being really small I knocked over 3 stacks of the drinks that had had the drink caps flying out, too.

SODA FOR YOUR SIR?

One time, a customer approached me and said he'd like to buy a bottle of drink, and the drink that he wanted was still wrapped in plastic, so, since he would just like a bottle, I had to cut open the plastic before I could retrieve that bottle. I wasn't concentrating while slicing the plastic as I was carried away by the conversation with a friend, and I never noticed that the plastic covering was joined closely to the plastic bottle, so as I was slicing through the outer layer of plastic, unknowingly I had also sliced through the bottle, before I knew it, the soda had splashed onto his face and the customer got a free facial wash! I felt bad, but the funny thing was that the customer himself was rather happy, so happy that he said in mandarin "showers of blessing!" Till today I'm still reminded of it each time I walk past a large tent that sells drinks.

Despite all the mistakes I made, I'm thankful that the floor manager kept giving me chances and looked out for me like a mother hen, whereas the supervisor of a certain heritage just enjoyed being a sick chicken, running her mouth all the time and threatening to dock my pay, but yet the floor manager, a really nice lady, stood up for me saying, "Are you crazy? You know how much these poor kids earn despite working so hard and you want to dock their pay?"

Then I was paid only $5 per hour, it was a really tough laborious job. Sometimes I wonder if it was the job agents who took home great commissions and left us with bare minimum. I know everyone's got to make a living, but seriously, if you should become a job agent in the future, spare more thought for the poor kids slogging just to earn some cash. At times I really did feel like giving up, I once got hit in the back by a pallet jack. I was transporting some goods and out of nowhere, an old lady decided to show up and, for no apparent reason, she knew that at the speed I was going I would never be able to stop in time, and this old lady of all things she had, she had no common sense! Instead of giving way to me, she proceeded to walk across my path, and I knew that if I didn't stop the pallet jack from hitting her she'd die and then I'll die (not literally, but you get the idea). So the only choice I had was to turn my back against the pallet jack handle to try to stop it. I did manage to stop the pallet jack; however it was at a cost, I got hit in the spine by the mental handle and, trust me, you wouldn't want to experience it.

Through this I learned the meaning of hard-work because not only was the condition inside the erected tent hot, it was really dusty, and by the time I ended work, my red company T-shirt had patches of black and white as a result of the dust and the mixture of my perspirations. It was also here that I learned for the first time that hard work really makes you attractive. The manager of the supermarket outlet came up to me a couple of times asking me to work for them once my current contract ended with the job agent, he said he really liked me because I was really hardworking.

ONE OF THE LARGEST FURNITURE STALLS IN THE WORLD

I've even worked in one of the world's largest furniture store! I've learned that for a company to grow large, is to minimise cost – including the pay of your workers. I know it sounds like I'm bashing them but it really doesn't feel good to get paid only $5 per hour watching over the entire section of kitchen equipments and utensils within a warehouse. It was about the size of a basketball court with countless cook wares, I had to re-arrange everything to ensure that the products were displayed nicely as well as attend to customers – and as you know there are customers who'd ask countless questions and buy nothing, and it got to a point whereby there were so many customers I got overwhelmed, the main bulk of my time wasn't arranging furniture but rather attending to customers. However, I met this lady who taught me to "always look up" whenever I got lost, and lookout for distinctive displays to locate where I am or plan to go to because the area was so huge getting lost was the easiest thing to do unknowingly.

TAX REFUND

I did this part-time job for a period spanning two years. I was a Queue-minder for this tax refund company; this meant I had to ensure that all particulars for refunds by the customer were filled in correctly before they could get their refund. I was recommended for the job, or rather even before I got the job I already had been noticed by the manager. Prior to this job, I did a surveying job for the same company, and the manager was more than happy with the results. This job really allowed me to see and hear stories of how the rich spend their money; I've seen the American Express Centurion as well as getting the chance to hold a Vacheron Constantin Malte Tourbillon watch. As a fan of luxurious watches I would say it was quite an experience.

The process for refunding was more taxing then. There wasn't much automation like today that helped quicken and streamline the process, so much so, that when I look back I felt like one of those pioneers. I know it doesn't sounds very believable but today there are no more Q-minders. Because you do not have to fill in any particulars but rather just head straight towards the counter, have your receipts scanned to verify the validity with your passport and you get your refunds. Therefore you do not need people to remind customers to fill in their refund forms, and generally I'm sure humans are smart enough to queue up in line accordingly. When I first started working there, customers had to fill in every single particular of theirs on the refund slip, such as full name, date of birth, full address including building and street names and numbers, the country the visitor was from and as well as two signatures on the slip. This was one of the problems because imagine if you had to fill in twenty pieces of such forms. Not to mention twenty, even by writing it five times will get you frustrated. And certainly it was for me and for the customers. Imagine on my part, repeating the same thing a couple of hundred times a day, and at times I had to say the same thing five times to the same customer. You know how irritating it is to repeat the same thing within a few minutes? It's like talking to a wall! Sometimes it was a language barrier, other times the customers just couldn't care less, and thought that regardless or not they'd still be getting their refunds, which wasn't true. Because I did my job to ensure that almost all things were filled in before they could approach the counter for their refunds. Or else I'd prompt them to go and fill in before coming back, and this was important, too, because it made the counter-staff's job easier. I mean it's already tough enough to ensure that they refund the correct amount to the customers, let alone asking them repeatedly to fill in the forms. On my part, I try to minimise the number of customers having forms that are incomplete. I'm human, too, and when traffic volumes are high it's easier to lose focus. However, should they refund the wrong amount, if there is a shortage, these poor ladies who work long hours with average salaries will have to pay for the loss. If it is a small amount it's fine, but on average the daily refunds would be hundreds of thousands, and, at times, millions, too, and all it takes is either a decimal place or zero to destroy their salary. It could be a week or even months.

During peak periods, even taking water breaks were difficult despite having a water cooler some thirty meters away. I remember there were times whereby the length of the queue would be estimated to be eighty-meters long from the time I start work till the time I end work, and you're looking at some eight to ten hours a shift, a few days in row that are like that. There were days that I worked up to 16 hours. Sometimes when I reported to work, and seeing such a huge crowd I honestly have thoughts of running home! However, I still learned a lot about crowd management! And I didn't even have time to read "Crowd management for Dummies" (Now I feel so smart I didn't even have to go to school to learn such things.) But really with regards to managing crowds I have only three things to share: keep calm, handle each individual one at a time and keep going.

Not only were my legs tired but my throat was sore too. And it's normal for customers to feel agitated because the queue is so long, and sometimes more than often we'd have customers trying to cut queue, insisting that they're late. It's rare if we ever let them jump the queue. Our reason? If you'd know your departure is at a certain timing, it's only right that you come in earlier to get your refunds, and if I let you jump the queue, what about everyone else? However we do make certain exceptions, it all boils down to the way they talk to us. Yes I know it sounds wrong and mean, considering that we should put customers first, but you're talking about people who'd jump the queue and creating a scene. Of course in the eye of the public we're wrong, but at the end of the day we're humans too, the only difference is that we're currently working else I guarantee you the staffs certainly would like to give you a piece of their stressed minds too.

But it was through this job that I was reminded— hard work makes you attractive to those around you. It was here that I found favor through sheer hard work with my colleagues minus a few, it's normal not to get along well with some people at work. Some may like you at the start but may eventually dislike you. The manager really liked me then, I was told that of all those that came before me, he never once praised them, and my colleagues have often asked for me to stand in during peak hours, or exchange shift with my peers. One of my fondest memories of a compliment was "thank God it's him, or else we'll be having a super long day!" I do not know that if it had to do with the fact that all of the contract staffs were females or I just happen to be a lady killer! Just teasing; favor and hard work always goes hand in hand.

Once I had a dispute with the job agent who said I was asking for too much when I asked for a pay raise, she said "it's such an easy job, and your pay is already quite good. There are always people such as the older generation ready to take your place and at any time of a call they could come down and work!" I did this job while studying and thus did not have the luxury of "coming in when needed" and besides, it took me some one hour and thirty minutes from school just to get to my working place. My colleagues, on the other hand, often tell me "why not ask her to come down and try? I bet she'll leave within an hour! If this was an easy job, many part-timers would not quit." So I upheld my dignity, and told the agent, "Okay fine, I'll leave at the end of two weeks, as stated in the contract." The minute I hung up, I approached the manager, told him of the situation and immediately he said "okay, sure, I'll hire you directly to work without the agent." To me, I uphold myself with respect and give whatever I have for my work, and I think that is the reason why people are more than willing to have me work for them. Though I did not take the job offered, which was to continue being a Queue-minder, or to work at the counter giving refunds, because I felt it was too much stress for me to handle. The money that I would be dealing with daily would be too much to handle, and it was through this that I also learned not to get enticed by money, but rather see it just as a transaction medium and nothing more. Because I knew if I focused solely on getting money all my life, I will lose it instead.

Weeks later, the agent called me back asking thrice if I'd like to come back to work with an increase of my pay. But more than anything here; more than standing my own ground, sometimes if it's possible to mend the relationship; if it doesn't cost you anything, do it. In spite of whatever happened between the agent and me, today we are still friends, we are still in contact and talk about various life issues. I don't let one small event dictate my future dealings with her, because I also understand where she came from, even though she may be wrong. But I learned to just move on.

BAD CUSTOMERS ARE A DAILY AFFAIR.

Though there were countless bad customers, I only remembered a few because they were outstanding for the wrong reasons. Before I go into detail, there is a disclaimer, I have to say again that whatever is written in this book is my own opinion, and I do not represent anyone but myself, with that said I am not saying that any company shares the same view as me. With every depot come different kinds of customers, but, sadly, the majority of the bad customers came from the smallest depot with the largest depot having the best customers. And the volume of customers varied greatly, too. The smallest depot had the most number of customers getting their refunds.

Affair #1

On one occasion while I was working at the smallest depot, the queue was so long it literally blocked the entrance of the other shops. And imagine being all alone dealing with the whole crowd and it is already annoying enough to compete with them in terms of their volume yet I still have to attend to customers who are literally shouting for help, please I'm not your dog. So this lady called me and I attended to her, her issue? She didn't have a pen to fill in her particulars so I lent her my pen, minutes later when I went back looking to retrieve my pen from her, she said, "Oh I threw it on the floor because I didn't know where I was supposed to put it." And I'm thinking, you're one fry short of a happy meal. It's horrible isn't it? The least she could have done was to hold onto it as she had to wait some time before she got to the cashier, or she could have at least returned my pen to my colleague.

Affair #2

On another occasion at the smallest depot, with the queue being equally long, this lady from a huge country dragged me aside and asked me to help her fill in all of her refund forms, of roughly twenty pieces. In my mind I was thinking, you're mentally interesting. Should I also be getting a cut of your refund? After telling her nicely, "Sorry, miss, I'm not able to help you, but I could certainly guide you." To my horror she stomped across to a shop and shoved all of their products off their shelves, just so she could make space for her forms and herself. This was insane, I mean, any human beings with common sense would certainly know that it is wrong to just shove other people's things aside; even a kid would know that, but not this crazy woman. I looked over at the sales person and I felt sorry, but, to my surprise, she said, "I know how you feel, honestly, I feel sorry for you; as for the bags, I can easily pick them up and display them again, but you've to deal with such people the whole night."

Affair #3

This time an incident occurred at the largest depot. Though there wasn't any queue this time, this male customer tried to be a pushover, he refused to fill in his particulars, and demanded an immediate refund. When told by my colleague that he had to fill in his particulars before he could get a refund, he got angry and started hurling vulgarities and threatening my colleagues at the counter who were all females in their late 40s to 50s. And all this happened while I was away on a toilet break, so on my way back, I saw from afar what had happened. I immediately thought to myself, *this guy is so lucky he met me, I feel like I could really help him.* So I walked over to him, and told him firmly, "Sir, if you refuse to fill in your forms completely, then you shall not get your refund, and I also saw how you treated my colleagues. If I were you, I'd apologize to these ladies like a man, or else they have the right to reject your refund for threatening them. Also, should they wish, they could get the Police to come down and settle this issue. Your choice, sir, you decide." You know it's almost like a David and Goliath thing. The guy was twice my size, one-and-a-half head taller than me. But I don't blame him for trying his luck to intimidate me. I mean, my clothes covered up each and every pound of pure muscle, so I guess he really didn't know what he was getting himself into. And, surprisingly, after what I told him, it didn't take him very long to decide to behave. It's like the elevator has finally reached the top, not even re-appeared, because I really had a hard time imagining him with a working brain. (Okay, I know you're thinking I'm very mean and nasty, but I've never said I was a nice guy)

After he filled in the form, he was still quite angry, and I guess he really tried to show his might, because he could not get back at us, so he tried to mess up our working area by littering all over the area. He left his cup on the table, threw paper onto the floor, this guy is literally asking for a fight. As he was about to walk off, I called him back and said, "sir, if you do not remove your rubbish and dispose of them accordingly, I'd like to remind you that there are at least a dozen cameras watching this now, and I'm sure, should the police come down, you'll have nothing in your defence." From his facial expression I knew he was boiling and he would have punched me, too, I saw him clench his fist. Actually, I thought I was doing him a favor indirectly, too. At the back of my mind I was thinking, Come on, go ahead, punch me. I'm sure you'll get an extension of your holiday, and a memorable free stay inside the lock-up area of the police station. Such an opportunity for a once in a lifetime stay in a world famous prison why not?

My thought on this affair? So what if you wore branded clothes from head to toe? Countless people wear the same brand as you, it doesn't help that your attitude and character fail to match that of the brand's value and goodwill.

Affair #4

This guy, apart from complaining about the long queue and the hassle, had a raging personality, too. When I approached him, trying my very best to persuade him to fill in his forms before he could get his refund, he shouted at me, "Why is your government so troublesome? I have a lot of money. I can even give your government money! Such a waste of my time." With that, I left him hanging alone. I told my supervisor about it, and we just laughed it off internally. But amazingly, after he felt that his childish acts could not do him any favors, he joined back into the queue and got his refunds, but, of course, grudgingly. Honestly, I didn't really care because there were so many people that needed my help and I would rather help.

Affair #5

"Customers are the reason why you have jobs, so you better learn to have more respect and treat them nicely!"

My grave offence? I approached this guy and said, "Hi, can I help you?" and then he replied "You're very rude, customers are the reason why you have jobs, so you better learn to have more respect and treat them nicely!" Personally I thought the best way to ensure that customers filled in their forms to ensure a smoother process was for me to approach every one individually and explain the requirements. On top of it, I thought if I created a lighter atmosphere, whereby everyone is more relaxed things would be better. I did the same thing with at least 30 other customers in the same line, and no one complained apart from him, in fact I had been greatly thanked by the passengers for easing their situation. I don't know if I was wrong or was he just crazy. You tell me. However the main reason was because it would save every individual at least some 30 seconds, and if you were to multiply that with the number of customers that period, it could easily save everyone an hour.

Not to be carried away or outdone by that crazy man (I mean it's important not to lose your joy over something small, but even more important to have fun, laugh things off, and have a great day at work) when he approached the counter to receive his refunds, at the next counter another lady whose refund was much more than the amount of the guy. And I really needed to get things off my chest fairly, but I couldn't start a verbal war with him nor could I give him a physical KO, so I did things "nicely" and I didn't even have to use a single finger. I approached the lady, smiled, and said "Wow madam, you're really fantastic, I mean it's so rare to have people like you who are not only nice but yet humble at the same time" (By now the guy knew that his refunds were way smaller than the lady because though he reached the counter later than the lady, he received his refunds with my colleagues still calculating the amount of that lady). With that I glanced across towards the guy, smiled and walked off. Obviously he was lost for words, he was so embarrassed he left in a hurry. The thing I like to point out here is – treat those serving you with respect, they are humans too. If you're not careful you'll lose more face than you can ever imagine.

Affair #6

Nothing much other than hearing from my colleagues that a female colleague got slapped in the face. She was deemed "rude" by a customer. This customer accused the girl of making her daughter cry and making her look bad when she was asked repeatedly to have her form filled in completely before she could be given a refund.

And guess what? Nothing was done to protect the poor girl. Not even a warning to the customer who gave the slap.

Affair #7

The queue was really long, and then out of nowhere I had customs officers appearing with a delegate's passport. They asked to jump queue as the delegate was about to miss his voyage. And, of course, no one likes having anyone, even a delegate, jump their queue, so this customer started getting violent and pushing me around. But thank God, the officials stepped in and told the guy, "If you get any more physical or abusive towards any of the staff here I'll have you arrested." That was sweet revenge!

In closing, for the bad customers, I once had a customer bark at me and insisted that I tell the guy in front of him to do the same thing, which was to stand in line before telling him what to do. In my mind I was thinking "Oh my God, are you an overgrown childish kid stuck in a 40-year old's body?" I cannot believe that such childish people are on the earth. Anyway, all I want to tell you, if you are a customer, be nice because it really isn't easy to cater to everyone with equal energy, effort, or mood. We who do customer services are humans too, and we certainly have days whereby we do not feel like working. We have our bad days, but we still try our very best to provide you services with the best of our efforts. If you think it is hard for you to fathom, imagine that it was your child serving you. If you still have trouble changing your mind-set, I hope you'll be able to find some balance up there soon.

GOOD CUSTOMERS

Good customers are few, but really easy to remember, especially those who tip you. I have had more than one regular customer coming up to me a few times to greet me. But also, this job taught me how the rich can be so humble and filled with humanity. I guess those with real riches are more likely to treat others with respect because they understand that whatever they have is temporal and that it is only on "loan" to them. Whereas the poor rich people are those who have some money but have more pride and insecurities to cover, therefore they come off as having money but no humanity or likeable character.

Though I cannot recall many good "affairs," probably because the bad ones were so good I could only remember them. I always remembered how customers would come up and tell me "You're doing a great job, keep it up!" Yes, it sounds common and normal, but try doing that for the person serving you next time, be it getting coffee or a snack. Do it especially when the queue seems never ending, and greet them with a warm smile. Trust me, not only will it brighten up their day, but the goodness will always come back to you, it's likely that they will treat you better. And should you see a customer bullying the person who attends to you, help him, it'll be greatly appreciated, because in the eyes of many, customers are forever right until they take the place of the server. It is not true that customers are always right; servers have their basic human rights, too. If you say that it is not true, should we then remove your basic rights when you're at work?

I remember it was during this job that I saw a legless cleaner crawling on the ground just to clean the toilet. It wasn't very easy to stomach, people talk about the flaws of the minimum wage and why it isn't good because it makes people lazy. I know there is no perfect system in the world. However, more should be done for these lower-wage poor people. No one really cares about how much these elderly people are earning – simply because those who do not care are those whose parents and grandparents are not going through what these poor folks are going through. If you ask me, I think these people are severely underpaid and on the other end those that blabber against this are severely overpaid. Swap places for a day and see how it's like.

LOCAL DRINK COMPANY

I worked for them for a few events and I really enjoyed working for them simply because the boss trusted me and she was really good at looking out for my welfare.

AN AMBUSH

My very first job with them was to "ambush" the public with their new soy bean drinks. We went to different marketplaces by being transported at the back of a lorry and we couldn't even tell where we were going. It was pitch black with only a glimpse of light, I felt like furniture and somewhat of an animal back then. Then, of course, once you start giving out free drinks, you didn't need to find the crowd, the crowd will find you. My friend and I first started carrying bags filled with drink packets, but it got to a point whereby the stock had been depleted even before we could reach places where there was a larger crowd. We ended up just asking the patrons to queue up for these drinks. At one place, we nearly had a fight with an elderly man, he didn't want to queue and insisted that because of his age he couldn't care less, he tried to snatch the drinks from us and he hurled vulgarities at my lady supervisor. Shame on that old man! It was not the first time we had encountered such customers but he just took things to a higher level. The funniest part? He performed some martial art stance and challenged us to a fight. My take home lesson? A good laugh, I laughed so badly I couldn't even fight him even if I wanted to. It is a tough thing to do, imagine half of you wants to stand up and protect your colleagues and give the dude a Knock Out punch and the other half just can't stop giggling. What would you do?

Months later my job agent called me up asking if I was keen to work with the same company for another project as I had left a great impression. They said they picked me instead of my friend to come back to work for them because I was hard-working and he was more concerned about being vain. (Zen if you're reading this, don't take it too hard, we were 17 back then).

SPORTS CARNIVAL

I did two annual events for them while I was studying. The job was simply to sell drinks to patrons, but the problem was that we had a huge amount of drinks to sell over the three-day period per event. Since it was a runners' event with the main chunk of patrons being runners, I decided that I'll sell them drinks in bulk, not by a bottle at a time because it would be too exhausting. So my strategy was to capitalize on the cost savings. Because the 500ml bottles would be sold at $1, and the 1.5 litres bottle would be sold at only $1.50, I told them that as runners it's a great deal because not only is it cheaper but you also get to buy a product that has way lesser sugar as compared to other drinks, plus if they'd buy a carton they would have saved $6 if they had bought a carton of big bottles as to the smaller bottles. Customers were more than happy to buy and buy more, because I told them if they were to buy two cartons and above I'd personally carry the drinks to their vehicles and would have more freebies for them. You see, customers love to hear how much they can save and what you as a sales person can do for them. On top of that, the key would be to handle the customer's children first; because once you get their attention you get their parents' attention as well. Though the drinks were heavy it was well worth it, my partner and I managed to clear three days of stocks within two and a half days. I have to also say that when working at such event jobs, it's important to have mutual understanding and proper communications with your partner. Each has to know his or her role, as well as helping the other party whenever needed, because not only does it make life easier for both of us, it builds trust, and as I've said with trust a lot of things become easier. The more selfless you are, the better things get. At certain time of the day I'd be bored and tired because there're weren't too many customers so I ended up making friends with people from the other booths and also sampling their products. I remembered once, somebody just walked over to my booth and gave me a carton of Vitamin Cs. That is one of the benefits of making and having friends, but still it's crazy because within that one carton I had like 30 bottles of Vitamin Cs!

MASCOT

Twice they got me to be their mascot for two very different events. It was a well-paying job but it was tough because it was extremely hot inside the mascot outfit and then on top of it you have the scorching sun. Before

I don the mascot outfit, I had to put on this inner wear, and boy just by wearing the inner wear, I perspired already, it was as if I had ran out of a shower without drying myself. The material was horrible; the only good part was that it made me perspire easily. And because of my stature; I'm 5ft 5 while the mascot was something like 6ft? I had difficulties walking about in the outfit, you know it's like wearing something that's way bigger than you and that the support inside of the outfit was so rough it caused me great abrasions on my shoulders. For my first event, things were better, it wasn't that physical as to my second event. At the soccer events, those rude kids just couldn't keep their hands off me, they seemed to enjoy pushing me, and trying to throw out freebies into the stands with most of your arm movements being reduced as a result of the outfit is strenuous, because I couldn't throw things very far. Either way, I realized that I wasn't animated enough to be a mascot, I didn't have too many moves or actions.

Overall, I was really happy working for them, their staffs trusted me and were confident with my decisions. They were open and asked for my opinions on how to make things better, which I'd say, is amazing because you rarely hear managers and supervisors seek the counsel of someone way younger and has less experience. On top of it, the manager was really generous, with each event; she'd buy tons of cakes for us as she was concerned that we might be too busy to eat. I know it's normal to have breaks but having your boss buy you boxes of food is not something I'd take for granted. During my Shape Run carnival, my partner and I had about 48 bottles of drinks to us over the three days. Just imagine how generous they were towards us! At the start of this job, I was hired through a job agent for them, but was hired directly by them after the first job, they waited for the contract duration of six months to end before looking for me personally. It wasn't a bad move, they ensured that on their part that they did not break any rules or go against any clause between them and the job agency.

BANQUET SERVER

I guess working at a banquet for hotels is a common job done by many teenagers, the money was alright and time passed really fast because you're always busy either with serving or clearing plates. At the same time you got to experience what it's like to serve at people's weddings apart from being served all the time when you attend a wedding. So I worked for two posh hotels.

I'M AN AH BENG? (GANGSTER IN SINGLISH)

Firstly, I know Singlish is not even a word; it's a term, a unique term used to describe the language of Singaporeans. It's unique because you can only find it here in Singapore, it is a mixture of different languages and they are fused together.

Working hours at the hotels were long, sometimes we worked up to 12 hours or more. It was a mundane job, just like every other job, however, because this is where people can really learn the meaning of "true colors" or "behind the scenes." You know it's funny how these posh hotels look so grand with hotel staffs smiling at you, ready to greet you. Yes, I know, it's all part of hospitality and, as they always say, "when your customers are happy, everyone's happy." So my first ever banquet job was with a friend who brought me in because they were lacking manpower. My friend taught me the basics, how to tie a ribbon behind the chairs for weddings, how to serve the guests, you know you've got to have some style in serving when you're working at a posh hotel. I was taught to slice and serve fish by using a spoon and a fork with the spoon below, all by just using a hand. I struggled with it, because I wasn't a great hands-on person, I guess, but here comes the reason why I was called an ah beng.

The first time I reported for work, I had dyed hair (well it was the school holidays and so I thought it was cool to mess around with my hair), it had shades of brown and, of course, what they were looking for was the standard black hair, black spectacles, presentable hairstyles, and trimmed finger nails. I passed all except for the hair issue, they handed me some gel and I was instructed to comb my hair in a certain style so that it would like it's black from different angles. I mean, come on, no one's blind, but maybe the manager was I guess? That night they decided to close an eye because they were really lacking manpower. So here we are clearing up the tables after a wedding to prepare for the next event tomorrow. And, as I was clearing, this manager, this foul-mouthed manager who seemed to be in his 30s kept shouting at everyone, and he was like, "Come on, Kieroy! Hurry up! Even my grandmother works faster than you." (Every mother's son seems to use the grandmother excuse to "motivate" people, but it's futile) I was still alright with it. I guess it's partly because of his job to ensure a quick turnaround and, more importantly, I believe it was part of his stinking personality. After we were done for the day, during the debrief, he went to my friend and said, "You better tell your ah beng friend, if he wants to come back tomorrow he better dye his hair black or forget about coming back." There are two pointers here. Firstly, I was present when he told my friend that comment about my hair. In my mind I thought, disgusting fellow, you've no guts to even say it to my face. But the funny thing was that he called me a gangster when he seemed as though he was born as a gangster, for every ten words he spoke seven were vulgarities, and he calls me a gangster? In my mind I was thinking to myself "amazing job old man." Still, I seem to always gain with most jobs I did, I always enjoyed making friends, talking to people and sure enough I started getting to know the chefs and, as you know, once you're in their good books, it's like they're your personalized chefs; they'd give you some extra food, teach you some stuff and, man, it was well worth it. And, oh, did I mention about how dirty they were? I remember once a piece of vegetable dropped on the dirty kitchen floor. The floor was stained with shoe marks and it was wet. I told the manager about it, and, to my horror, he picked the vegetable up from the floor, put it back onto the serving plate and told me to serve it. There you go ladies and gentlemen, value-added food for you, courtesy of the hotels where you've been eating.

But through this experience, I got to understand and see first-hand that, once you're out there working, no one really respects you, if you come off as soft, game over. Getting shouted at isn't meant for everyone, but everyone needs to at least experience it a few times so that they may know that things do not come easy in life, and therefore appreciate things more. Though it's unruly to shout (come on we aren't barbarians) but it certainly would wake up your idea of "work is easy, it's a breeze all the time."

COFFEE, TEA, OR ME?

I never thought that after such a horrible experience I'd still be working at a hotel again. But this time, things were much better. I took up this job partly because I could have more time to help my relative with his car business, but it was a tiring one. Because I had to report to work by 6:45 a.m. I woke up at 5 a.m. just to prepare breakfast and then rush off to work. But by doing so, I felt sick, emotionally. Boarding the first bus at 6 a.m. to the interchange, I saw kids who were between 7 to 10 years old sleeping on board these buses with schoolbags that seemed way bigger than their body frame. At that point, I thought to myself, "Why bring kids to this earth to go through such a tough life? I mean, things are probably not going to get better with inflation rising faster than the majority of the pay earners, and, honestly, the GDP is a poor indicator of the status of the people of the country. People always talk about the rich living the "life," you rarely hear stories of the poor who struggle just to meet their daily needs." Life is already so tough on most working adults, but yet even the kids are not spared. I do agree that it's good to teach kids to wake up early to make full use of the day, but this is extreme in a first world country. It's pointless to talk about third-world countries and their struggles here, because what we want is to do our best for our own kids, kids of our own nation, not compare which country has the worst standard of living or quality of life.

Anyway, back to my working experience at this renowned hotel. It was an easy job, at the start of the day I had to wipe down the tables to ensure it was clean, bring out the coffee and tea pot as well as to ensure that things were in the right place. I was mainly serving and refilling customers' drinks and the clearing of their plates during the breakfast hour, I got to admit that standing for hours with two jugs of drinks inside a metal flask is straining on the forearms. Sometimes my hands would go numb from carrying them for too long. After the breakfast ended, I had to prepare the table for tea time with new sets of cutleries. I realized that the people working were extremely particular in the way things were laid, for example even the towels had to be folded in a certain way and the plates had to have their design shown in a certain way.

A worldwide Beer Distributor

So when I finally hit 18, more jobs were available to me, and I decided to try out different jobs.

Beer promoter

I did a couple of beer promoting jobs for this company during the festive seasons and there wasn't anything fascinating, just a couple of jobs to earn some bucks.

Beer merchandiser

I had to travel from various supermarket store outlets in a day to refill and sort out the beers from the shelves. This means that I would need to go to the storeroom where they kept all the beers and refill the beers on the shelves so the public could buy them, I had to also arrange the beers according to their expiry dates, with the earlier dates at the front of the shelves and the latest at the back. It was physically draining as well, because beers aren't light and to carry out and stack these beers climbing up and down was exhausting. Every day I would have at least five different locations to go. However, the main issue wasn't traveling or carrying beers that made it hard, it was working with a female supervisor. Again, I'm not sexist, however, when I took on this job the job agent had told me beforehand that the previous guy for the job left only after a few days, and had a poor attitude towards work; therefore, causing the supervisor to have a bad impression of guys ever since, and, unknowingly, I took the bullet for the last guy. (Ladies, please do not make the man in front of you pay for the crimes committed by the boy before. It's crazy no matter how you look at it. Please stop.) While working with her she'd always grumble about how slow I was, and that I had a poor attitude at work. This is rare because out of the many jobs I did, this was the rare few complaints that came against me. I remember one time as I was carrying out beers from the store, I asked her politely to move aside, as I did not want to hit her due to the small constraints of the aisle inside the store. Also because she had repeatedly complained about having severe backaches. Instead of moving aside, she fired back at me, "There's so much space, can't you just go through? And by the time you're done it'll be very late already." With that I bit my tongue and didn't want to fire back, but two days later I resigned. I called up the agent with whom I have had positive feedbacks from former employers who reported that I've been so good that they want me back for whatever jobs they had, if possible. I told the agent "hey you know, we've been working together for so long and you've rarely hear people complain about me, so I don't think the fault lies with me but her and I do not wish to work with her any further." True enough, the agent agreed and I left.

AIR CONDITION SALESMAN

I took up this job just so I could pay for my driving license; this means that for every lesson I took I had to work two days just to pay it off. It was a grueling job, every day after school I would climb up and down countless flights of stairs of HDBs and it was draining. Though we would generally take the lift to the top floor and then take the stairs downwards, it was exhausting on our bodies; our knees and our throats especially since we were always running and speaking to customers. During my five hours of work nightly, I would have distributed flyers and knocked on an estimated 300 to 400 units of flat with my buddy only to be rejected ninety eight percent of the time. This figure isn't even exaggerated and you think getting rejected by a girl is bad? We all need money to survive and, honestly, love without money is nothing. Looking back now I guess it made me more resilient whenever I faced rejection; I can take rejection in the face because it's not a big deal to me now.

Our job was to sell our air-con services such as steam cleaning or chemical washing. In general, people do have their regular service staffs to maintain their air-con so not too many people were keen. But even if they were, they were rather sceptical as steam cleaning was not as popular as it is today. Even so, when I was doing this job there were countless other companies offering the same kinds of services with competitive rates, making things more challenging. Back then people would likely get their air conditioners cleaned during the rainy days as they had to rinse the condenser and compressor which were located outside the balcony of the flats thus causing the water to drip towards their neighbours below, thus the reason for cleaning only during raining days.

With steam cleaning you could do it anytime at any weather conditions, we had equipment that could generate high heat to kill 99% of germs, and it was a quicker, cleaner and more efficient job. The coils of the air con would have no jelly like substance; as they would be flushed out. And with just one look at the air-con we could easily tell the problems causing it; such as a lack of gas thus resulting in the air con not being to perform at its peak. In fact air cons are able to last between 10 to 15 years that is something many people do not know. They generally think it can only last up to ten years. At the end of the day it's all about maintenance; if you do it regularly then it's only normal to have it functioning in the long run; that is, of course, unless you get a subpar contractor to maintain your air con. My advice? Clean it once a year with chemicals and wash the filters every three months, this way it would help reduce your electricity bills. As for recommending a reliable brand, I would say Mitsubishi.

HAVE YOU SEEN THE AIR-CON BOY?

We would comb some five blocks per night; and on Saturdays things got crazier. The only thing I remembered about my buddy was that he was a "crazy dude who worked like his life revolved only around work." His day job already requires him to move around as he was selling photocopy machines and at night he would work the extra job, though we both had crazy work ethics, the difference was that I was given a basic salary with commission while he was paid solely through commission. The commission was impossible to get because I had to clinch two deals in one night. And even if we could get a deal between the both of us each night it was considered as amazing already. It was anything but easy, and every time either one of us would strike a deal, I would always say "to your account" because I know it's harder on him. For this job, once the customer lets us into their homes to check on their air cons, and once we've diagnosed their problems, they are likely to sign a deal with us. I guess it's for either one out of these three reasons; it's either time for them to clean up their dirty air-cons, or we were both rather good sales people, or likely that they kind of pitied me because they could tell I was rather young, and they just gave in. Some customers were really nice, I remember this lady, she had two kids and her husband, who was a sole bread winner and a taxi driver. She was rather upfront about her financial situation; she told us that she would like to get her air-con cleaned as it was years since someone cleaned it, but they could not afford it. However, she invited us into her place, offered us food and drinks, I guess she could tell we were exhausted, too. But it is such small things; small acts of kindness that keeps people going.

On Saturdays we would usually go to older housing estates such as Toa Payoh or Hougang. I hated both places. For Toa Payoh we would go to blocks that were thirty stories high, the tough part was because each floor only had some two or three units, and it would mean that we would be hitting the stairs very often, faster than what we would like to, and thus tiring out easily. For Hougang, I remember how complicated the building structures were; some elevators could only go to some floors, and some floors had no elevators; it was like a maze. I spent most of my energy trying to figure out how to maneuver around the blocks instead of selling the air con services. One Saturday, we decided to try out at the estate of Pasir Ris, and it was a depressing place to be. We combed ten blocks, and not a single door opened! You got to know how frustrating it was, because, even on a bad night, people would at least open up and talk to us even if they were not interested to get their air con serviced by us, but on this day it was zero. That was when I learned that life is never fair; sometimes you try so hard, yet you're not even close to anything named a deal. But I guess life goes on, we just learn to laugh at the tough times, pick ourselves up and move on.

You think you're hot?

So often we hear people whine about not having enough air cons or the air con isn't cool enough, (I know I'm guilty of complaining) but do you know that even in Singapore where everyone thinks that just because of the beautiful buildings and high GDP that everyone lives in a comfortable and cool place to sleep. I bet you didn't know that there are people who have either only one old air-con for their entire house which they rarely use because they have no money to pay for or not even a single air con, and you have people who have three or more air cons in a room and still complaining about the lack of it. Before you say that we live different lives, think about what you have, and what they have not and then re-consider your words. Seeing all these poor people live their lives, in what, I believe is considered as poverty in Singapore, opened my eyes to see that in life it really isn't about competing to get more riches only for your selfish self, but rather what we can do even for our own country people who live really poor lives. It is different from those people who go around selling tissue-papers at hawkers and telling a fake pitiful story just so they can sell you some tissues. Yes, I believe there are genuine cases. But towards the manipulative cheaters, it's a shame that you carry yourself cheaper than the poor people who have dignities and the amount of money that you cheat others of, is the amount that you are only worth. I think it is a good experience for everyone to see how; not just hear of, or talk about, how these poor people live their life daily; it would certainly help to put our lives back into the right perspective and could reduce a whole lot of selfishness.

I seldom sleep with the air conditioner on, unless it is extremely hot, mainly for these reasons: firstly being in an air-conditioned room while at work is already bad enough as it dehydrates me internally and my skin. Many people are unaware that their body is losing a lot of water while they are sitting down for prolonged periods in an air conditioned room. Secondly, sleeping without it allows me to better acclimatise my body to the surrounding temperature, and I guess it's something not everyone can or is willing to do. Thirdly, it helps keep the earth going; as there won't be any CFCs coming from my air con. Therefore, by doing it I am actively making the world a better and greener place for the generations to come.

THE PRIDE KILLER

I think we grow the fastest when we do not allow our pride to be our own obstacle. I had so many doors being slammed in my face so many times I lost count, it wasn't even people slamming the door at me because of how I spoke, but rather the moment they saw me approaching their flats to give them a flyer, they just shut the door immediately.

There was a particular incident that smashed my pride then. I remembered giving a flyer to this kid and told him to pass it to his parents. A few minutes after I left for the other units along the corridors, he shouted for me, so I ran over, and before I could even reach his door step, I was two steps away, he dropped the flyer when I just reached out my hand to receive it but it was too late. It was an eye opener, because I was never treated this way before, and you thought it would only happen in drama shows, but it happened to me. I stood down, lowered myself to pick up the flyer off the ground and moved on. But it taught me a lot, just one incident taught me that pride is the real killer, pride comes before your fall, and it is your own pride that could eventually kill you if you can't suck it up and move on.

You know it was like one of those movie scenes with an arrogant boss, and in the scene the boss drops the money on the floor so that the waiter could pick up the money from the floor instead of a hand to hand transaction. It was like a kind of power play in the business world.

YES, YES, THEN NO

There are all sorts of customers, and it was during this job that I saw how customers can actually say yes, sign the deal (which is another yes), then back out and ask for their deposits to be refunded. Though we were initially pissed, but we came to realize that cheap people do not back their words up with actions. They gave all sorts of reasons, but what stood out among these reasons and excuses to me was the way they seemed so interested at first, and then saying things like "I will surely recommend my friends." This was when I realized that genuine purchasers are often those who spoke less, and asked few questions. They do not come off with an airy attitude, but rather just plain and simple "alright please help me deal with my air con." If you work in a certain industry for a period it's easy to pick up things such as sign of how customer give themselves away.

EXCUSE ME?

Along the way I've had some exciting encounters while doing this job. I once was greeted by a girl, I rang the doorbell, she opened the door but I was speechless! It's like seeing an angel from heaven, she looked really beautiful, it was like living in a dream, in paradise. I mean it's rare for me to go speechless, but it just happened to me that day. It took me a while before I could answer her when she asked what I wanted. I stuttered! Now looking back I think it was quite funny, but I guess it's normal to have days whereby the words just wouldn't come out. Another time, I rang the bell only to be greeted by a girl in a bikini and she was all wet! Upon seeing me, she shut the door, ran to grab a towel before coming back to open the door again. I thought, "Was she waiting for somebody?"

Once I chanced across two students sniffing glue at the stairs; when they saw me, they greeted me with the, "mind your own business, I can't even think straight now" look. They looked ready for a fight, but I wasn't even keen because I had to work; it's not my business to help everyone and I thought, I couldn't be bothered to get my hands dirty—should anything happen, I'll just call the police.

Speaking of the police, I ran into two loan shark runners. I remembered the both of them; a male and a female. Both were wearing a helmet to cover their identity. They were at the last unit of the floor, but the thing was that I needed to get past them, so that I could get to the staircase and then to the other floors. When I walked past the unit, I didn't even stop to hand out a flyer, but I did happen to exchange a couple of glances with both of them. They were harassing a family, and it was bad because there were kids in the house. Still I didn't get involved. But the funny part was when I looked down from the next building, not only did I see countless neighbours' heads sticking out the window, the two loan shark runners were seated down on the pavement surrounded by the police! (It's funny how you're cool one minute, and then you "freeze" instantly when the police shows up.)

On another encounter, while I was going from door to door, we noticed two girls from the block opposite; they were probably between the ages of 14 to 17. Both were either giving out flyers or sticking stickers on the doors of other residents. The only problem was that, when we went past the units they visited beforehand, we found out that they were actually distributing flyers that were for unauthorised money lenders; loan sharks. And there was a man looking out for them, I guess it was to make sure that they did their job as well as to look out for any police. To this, I think though the money was probably very good and attractive to these young kids, one should never be in this line, because if you get apprehended by the police, your future is ruined.

Making and selling mid-autumn festival moon cakes

I told you earlier about how hard work attracts people, now I'd like to add on that it open doors for you. The manager of the local drink company personally recommended me to the boss for this job. The best part? I got to negotiate a salary nearly 30% more than what was being offered to others working during the event. It was also here that I got to know owners of the other companies with a few asking me to join their company.

This was an exhausting job. I worked 12 hours a day every day for almost a month; I would have done a whole month if I wasn't given a medical certificate of 5 days as a result of an infected finger. (I would have gone on, I was tired but I certainly would have pressed on) I was on my feet the entire time I worked, the only time I sat down was to eat and it lasted only over an hour for the whole day. Every night after work, I wouldn't even have the energy to use the computer, it was that exhausting, 'cause all I wanted to do was to sleep and prepare for the next day's work. The first few days were tough because I had not stood so long in a while, it was nearly a year since the tax refund job that I stood that long, in reality there is no way to train yourself for such a job unless you are doing it regularly.

It was the first time I was actually learning to bake moon cakes from scratch and it was an experience. After trying my hands on to mould the dough as well as inserting the ingredients for the first few days, the chef and I decided that I'd probably be better off just weighing the dough, slicing it up and preparing it. (There you go again; I told you hands-on things are not my forte.)

Every morning I'd come in, prepare the ingredients for the day and then after I would clean the display glasses before we actually started baking them. The moon cakes sold by us were actually Teochew-style moon cakes; they tasted really good especially right out of the oven as it was really crispy. We'd bake the moon cake fresh daily and it was on display for customers to see as well. On average we would make a couple of hundreds, and the main ingredient was yam. Though it was a mundane process, all I have to say is that – as long as you have friends with you, life just becomes much better. For three quarter of the day I would mostly concentrate on baking the moon cakes and then selling them once we made enough for the day. It was a physically grinding time, as well as being a little messy; we had to deal with smashed yam, pumpkin, egg yolks, sticky dough and black sesame. This was the first time I was exposed to working in a kitchen; or rather it was a make-shift area for baking. There were many times we experimented on mixing the different types of flavors, some tasted good and some didn't. I was on very good terms with the Chinese chef, though he could hardly speak English, and I, on the other hand, could hardly communicate in Chinese. We had a great time talking about everything under the sun. At the start of the day we would account for the amount of moon cakes that were carried over from the previous day and would also plan for the number of moon cakes we would be making. But the best thing about him was that he told me "take as many as you like to bring home, then I will account for the reminder, as for those that you took. I'll just say they were used for sampling." (Amazing how good things happen when you're on good terms with the chef!) Then we gave samples without recording, until the boss's dad came down and passed the order that we were to account even for samples. I know it isn't right, not justifiable, but I guess it's part of working within the Food and Beverage industry to enjoy foods that are meant for others.

MANY MOUTHS TO FEED, TOO FEW HANDS

During the sampling period, we would slice up the moon cakes and leave it for sample. It was just that we never imagined the samples to finish each time we turned our backs to slice more. I was speechless. You know, the ratio of samplers to customers were like 25:1. On average we'd serve somewhere between the hundreds daily, and we tried our very best to give samples that were freshly baked but it was crazy at that time, so much so that we were mostly busy with slicing samples instead of selling them, people weren't really buying but rather free loading. I know it sounds bad, after all, the purpose of samples was for customer to sample our products. But not too many people were buying, I remember reading an article in a newspaper that said "Only 1 out of 10 customers were purchasing." It was that ridiculous! But I guess that was the reason why today, I'm not very keen on trying samples unless I'm really keen on buying, because I understand how tough it is to keep preparing samples for people without selling. I understand the rationale that people want to try before they can decide which brand to buy, that's totally acceptable, but coming back and grabbing a few pieces and not buying day after day tells me you're a cheap freak. Again don't get offended, it's just my point of view.

Anyway moving right along, deeper into the sampling issue, there was a certain lady who would come around every afternoon to sample every stall's moon cake, each time we asked if she was keen on buying, she'll either ignore us or just say, "later on, I'm still trying out." In my mind I was thinking, *Do you really know what you want? Will you really buy? Are you sure you know what tastes good after sampling every stall's product?"* There were at least 30 stalls and every stall had their prices displayed. So my colleague approached me one day and told me her "plan," and this was our conversation.

Colleague: "Hey, there's the same auntie again, go attend to her and I'll snap a picture of her!"

Me: "Err, okay, I'll do it."

(So the lady walks up, and she's a medical staff, she also had her name tag on)

Me: "Good evening, Madam, can I help you? These are some of the different samples of different flavors; we have yam, yam with pumpkin, yam with black sesame, and also the double egg yolk.

(I guess you could really tell that I was very into my job.)

Customer: (carries on eating without replying to me)

Me: "Madam, would you like a box of moon cake? Can I get you some?"

(By now my colleague got a picture of the customer up close and personal)

Customer: "No thanks, I'll buy another time."

After the lady left, my colleague approached me with the picture and asked if she should post it online. I told her, that if she wanted she could, but she should censor the customer's face and nametag from the picture and do not disclose any information that would get her into trouble. (Sometimes people judge others and say things like "how could you do such a thing?!" But really, when you're working for duration so long, you end up doing things just to make your day a little better. However, I know that it is still wrong to do such a thing, but we all learn through mistakes). Before I knew it, she was interviewed via phone and she disclosed the location and our working hours. (Honestly, it was as if someone set off a self-destruct time bomb on us.) Within hours, the post was viewed a few thousand times online. Not long after that she ended her shift and that was when our nightmare started. Hours later, I was about to end my shift, which leaves just two female part-timers to handle the closing. The angry lady customer together with her family came down to our shop, demanding that she know the girl who posted the photo as well as to see my boss. When I first saw the lady I thought, *this lady is really on fire, Imma leave and not get burned.* It was 9 p.m. and I called my boss. Within 30 minutes, she arrived. But it was an ugly scene to watch, seeing my own boss being berated by the lady in public. In my mind, though, I knew it was alright to leave, as I was just a part-timer, and it didn't concern me at all even if the company closed down the next day because I still have to be paid for working. However, in my own conscience I knew it wasn't right to leave my boss to fend for herself, as a man—despite being a powerless employee, I just knew that my presence made a difference. Imagine being in a public area and having an angry family surround you, kicking up a huge flame of anger and throwing it at you. It was crazy. Things were uglier than expected because the customer only found out through her friend, and she was told by her friend "Hey, you're online! And it says you're a stingy aunty!" Imagine receiving a text informing you of it. Not only will I be pissed, but I'll wear a mask wherever I go! Later on she claimed that she could not even leave home for work as she was too embarrassed to even see strangers let alone her colleagues. (I know it is wrong for the photo to be posted online especially with such an embarrassing caption, but honestly, after that incident I further believed in not being a cheapskate. Samples are meant to be sampled, but not meant to fill your stomach – that to me is one of the biggest issues we humans face today. We make ourselves look cheap, not because we cannot afford things, but we portray our life as cheap). The whole thing lasted for some twenty minutes, before my boss left for the company in charge of the website, in hope of removing the post made online. It was a really tough time for my boss, as she stayed up all night outside the press company just so she could ask them to take down the article the next morning; though the damage was done I was certain my boss went through hell. Imagine waiting in anxiety the whole night with thoughts of your business winding up over an incident which is not even caused by you, but your workers, and I guess things were much worse when it was your dad who handed over the business to you. Honestly, if the business winds up because of something small, I'll feel crappy and will not know how to explain it to my father who spent his life maintaining and preserving the company for the next generation). On our part, it was easy to tell that the photo came from our shop because of the angle it was taken from.

Though we knew things were escalated into a huge issue, we never imagined in our wildest nightmare that the management of the shopping mall would come to our store to question us about the issue. You know things are serious when you see people from the management come down to tell us to direct any question by the media to them. That day I remembered seeing media people with their camera crew and equipment going around to interview people about the issue, but, amazingly, I doubt they ever found out who it came from or what actually happened. I thought that was the end of things but I was so wrong, I heard later on that there were lawyer's letters being sent down with the intentions of banning the company from selling moon cakes anymore. Come to think of it, it's rather horrible because imagine losing out one of your biggest profit contributions, and then for many more years to come. I do not know what the outcome was; I'm guessing it was an out-of-court settlement. Today, the company still takes part in the annual Mid-Autumn Festival, but it was a crazy experience for me.

FATTENED WITH ARROGANCE

Though every company tries it's best to get sales from customers, I think in general everyone had a good relationship with each other, we greeted each other and spoke daily despite trying our best to get customers to purchase our products. But I could remember there was this particular stall; situated diagonally across from our stall, and this stall had a really arrogant staff member. First he paraded as though he was the boss, next he acted as though his business was very good of which it was nowhere close. Throughout the time of the entire event, I never once noticed anyone buying more than thirty boxes on average daily, and his stocks weren't even moving. Yet he had the audacity to come towards our stall and boast about how great his sales were. But I guess when people get bored and are jealous they tend to the stupidest and craziest things.

The most annoying part was that he kept taunting us with his sales and assumed that he could do whatever he liked, such as eating our samples as though they were his. On top of that he would always "order whatever stocks we had." With every passing time that he tried to irritate us with his antics, we would often smile and just let things go.

One day, things changed. I was pissed, because not only was he obstructing our business but he had irritated us to a point whereby a fight would start and when he decided to come over and "order all our stocks,"

I gave him more than he could ever bargain for. When he approached me, and asked me to write down on a memo whatever stocks we had as he'd like to purchase everything, I wrote him a memo that stated 30 boxes of moon-cakes, handed it to him, smiled and said "Okay, I'll pack every single moon cake in boxes for you personally once you come back and show us the receipt of the purchase." When I told him that, my colleague freaked out, he said Are you serious?! What if he really buys everything that you wrote? We don't even have so much stock on hand currently" To which I replied, "Don't worry, people like him talk more than they walk, else he wouldn't have a 40-inch waist-line!." True enough, the moment he received my memo, he tore it apart a few steps later, he wasn't even near the counter to make payment. I got infuriated. I then turned towards my colleague and said "I just prayed and asked God to make his business go down without any sales, just watch." I couldn't be bothered to get my hands dirty by punching him so instead I told God about my "situation" and He delivered With that I have to say that God is a righteous God who watches over and protects his own people; however we should try to pray for their salvation instead of cursing them, but I couldn't care less. God loves the sinner, but I'm more certain that He protects his own people in times of trouble. He is God and He can do whatever he likes. But the thing is this, when justice is done, it brings joy to the righteous, (those upright and who are in right standing with God) but to the evildoers it is dismay, calamity and ruin. True enough, his sales went from that few boxes to almost zero for a few days, Sadly I only got to hear the news of my prayer being answered as I was away on Medical Certificate for five days as a result of an infected finger with pus; it was the result of wearing gloves for too long and also likely because I wasn't hygienic enough. But anyway, when I got back to work, I noticed he had bruises on his eye. When I asked him about it, he said, "Oh, I walked into a lamp post." However, I believe it was otherwise; it was more likely that he got beat up outside as he had bruises on his arms as well. God is my witness, I never prayed for him to get beat up outside, nor did I succumb to unscrupulous means by getting people to teach him a "lesson."

After the episode, the guy seemed nicer. He seldom obstructed our business nor was he as nosy, he just minded his own business. One day he offered me some moon cakes; I believe he was trying to bury the hatchet.

Though I didn't take his offer, because I simply felt that my moon cakes were way better, it was only after this then did his business improve. I guess God had a clear message for me that day; it was on the seventh day since I prayed that the guy's business improved. Moral of the story? I guess it's safe to say that it's not a good idea to mess with me. People believe in using the higher authority, and I agree that it can do wonders. I personally believe in divine intervention; believing in the highest authority.

FATIGUE, THE CATALYST

Working for such a long period of time isn't easy, work is already difficult with the different types of working styles from different individuals and then when you add on fatigue; which is the main catalyst for a reactive chemical reaction between exhausted and moody people, things get chippy. I remember once, I had an exchange with a female colleague, an aunty who was between fifty to sixty years old. (Before you jump the gun and say I'm rude or I have no business having such an exchange because after all she's elderly and I should be giving in, please read on) For no reason she was the only one who kept jawing at me saying that I should sell moon cakes instead of joking around. I didn't know if it was because I kept joking with the chef or for whatever reason. On our part, we were tired, too; we were baking some few hundred moon cakes daily. And on top of that I also helped with the selling of moon cakes once we were done baking for the day; it wasn't like I sat around slacking. So I fired back and I said, "Well, it's such an easy job, and you should feel bad that I sell nearly more than you, despite spending most of my time baking moon cakes." She was left speechless, the rest of the staff took sides and surprisingly no one stood up for her; all of us were part-timers, some were 19, some were in their 30s but none stood up for her, so I guess they all kind of agreed with me because privately they told how manipulative she was, and that she was only good at bossing around.

REFLECTING OFF AS A FULL MOON

This job helped opened my eyes wider. Though I always knew that I was a people person or rather I had an Ambivert personality and had some leadership qualities; some that made people listen to me (I have to admit that there are many people who just cannot stand working with me or listening to the things I say, but I rather focus on the positive, the good results, instead of the few bad ones) I do not know if it was because I was charismatic or I had an aura; a leadership or maybe a commanding aura. But it was here that I further realized that I actually had the ability to lead people; people of different age groups. There were many times we had to make decisions on our own, either because we did not want to trouble the boss over something small, or we didn't have the time to call the boss. The main guidelines were stipulated, but, as we all know, regardless of the number of guidelines, there will always be vague areas, and that is when the workers have to decide. It should be safe to say that making decisions are easier when everyone is on board and supporting your idea, being confident with both presenting it to the team and trusting that things will work is what keeps things going. To the boss I believe that it would make her life easier, because they would rather have thinking workers who take initiatives.

I was really fortunate to have worked with people who would listen and just do the things that were needed, either because I said so, or they just knew how to take the initiative. Though we were all part timers apart from the chef; none had any rank or position higher than another, we all worked very well as a team. I think things become simple when you have a leader; either someone who just steps up, or maybe an appointed one, but I guess for this instance it was because I was the most outgoing and talkative one therefore I seemed to attract everyone's attention. All in all I believe that it's all about listening to one another, understanding where each is coming from and how we can all help to make not just that one individual's life better but all of us as a whole. This means no one complains about who does more or less, but rather what we can achieve. Looking back, I really feel that I was in many ways – reflecting the boss when it came to decision making.

SELLING OUT WITHOUT SAMPLES

You read it right. It was nearing the end of the event; the last two days of the event, and we had about some 100 moon cakes to sell, but at the same time we weren't keen to give out any more samples as it would cause us to lose out on the profits. My colleagues then egged me on saying, "Hey, quick work your Kieroy magic, do whatever you have to do and see if you can sell out these moon cakes." I thought it was a fun idea, it was challenging but I couldn't care less. So I dug my heels in and started promoting, with no samples given just purely selling. It was like literally testing my sales ability as well as my endurance because it sure wasn't easy especially with our competitors still giving out samples and larger discounts.

I solely relied on two factors; pointing towards the stack of empty trays and telling customers "look at how much we've sold; I'm afraid if you walk another round there will not be any left for you." With a smirk on my face that says, "You know I'm not kidding right?" (The key here was that I didn't say that the stocks sold were just for one day; alright I wasn't truthful but neither was I lying either. Here you go—sales without compromising your values through lying) With the other factor; building a good rapport by greeting them with enthusiasm; this itself already gave me an advantage over many who were either too tired or couldn't be bothered to entertain customers, and then when they bought some, I would subtly suggest "how about buying another box? It's only once in a year that you get to enjoy freshly-baked moon cakes from us, and I'll give you a little more discount." I remembered there was one particular customer, a lady; she asked me "What is the difference between your product and the competitors? They are even giving more discount than you." So I replied cheekily, "Well miss, the main difference is this, the female sales assistant isn't as good looking as I am." The outcome? I'll leave it to you to decide.

"Next" is the way to go

The main thing about upfront customer service, or sales for that matter I think every sales person must have the attitude of "next is better." Else the answer will forever be a "no" and you'll get demoralised very easily, imagine getting rejected ten times a day, it isn't that bad but imagine if it's a hundred or a thousand. What do you think your morale will be like? Do you think you'll be smiling? It's more likely you'll be depressed and ready to quit. It is not an easy task to do by having the "next" mind-set whenever you get rejected by a customer let alone persisting when a storm such as financial drought hits you.

When it comes to customers who are sincere and ready to purchase things based on my experience, the questions they ask are few, the best customers are those who just tell you what they want. And the questions asked by them will tell you how genuine they are. After trying a sample, it should be clear in their minds whether it is a yes or no, no maybe. A serious buyer knows what he or she wants, apart from the minor price difference which is negotiable and a deal will be imminent depending on how you pitch your sales pitch. Many times, it may not be about the product but about the sales representative himself. I once attended to a couple, when just a few sentences into our conversation the man asked, "Are you the boss? Because the way you present things, it's rather rare for workers to have such attitude" (Of course I was beaming with joy on the inside). The couple ended the conversation by telling me, "We'll come back later." To me I thought it was "just another customer" who would use it as an excuse not to buy. But I was wrong, moments later they came back, bought a few boxes and said "The only reason we buy from you is not because your moon cake taste the best, but rather because we love how you dealt with us." That made my day.

Miscellaneous jobs

Because I cannot write out everything; there's too much to be written, these are some more of the jobs that I've done, what I have here is probably ninety percent of what I did because I can't remember everything.

Selling washing machine detergent – It was a job that came out of the blue. A female supervisor whom I only worked with twice but rarely spoke to, gave me a call randomly, said she got my number from her former colleague and asked if I was keen to do the job. She said she couldn't find anyone else suited for such a job. In my mind I was thinking, "was it because it was a 'weird' job?" The job was easy, and it paid well, but it was just dead boring as there weren't many customers who were looking to buy washing machine detergent. I got so bored; I decided to help an old uncle carry rice sacks onto the shelves. It was tough on a sixty-year-old man to be carrying sacks of rice that were 10kgs, so I thought, why not, as I had a lot of free time. The key take away for this job; look busy, act busy, move around as though I had to re-stock. The store supervisor said I was really hardworking, but what he didn't know was that I spent time walking around the mall next door.

Local departmental store – The job scope was to pack goods at the counter after the cashier had scanned it, and I was to put it in a carrier for the customer. I could still remember, it was the first day of the many event jobs that I did with them, there were about thirty of us, a few were my friends since it was the school holidays we decided to work together. So we were told to wait in a room as the manager would like to brief us on the job. She came off with a stern look, one of those like your discipline mistress in school. The moment the manager walked in, she glanced across the room, and the very first thing that came out from her mouth was "Who's Kieroy?" At that moment I was giggling away with a friend, thinking, "This is crazy, why would she call me out?" So I stepped up and I said, "Here I am." After she had allocated us our positions and tasks, everyone was asked to report to our positions. As I was walking out, she called me and told me to stay behind. I thought it was strange, but she tried to get to know me. She said, "Your agent highlighted you personally for your work ethic to me apart from the rest, so I thought you must be really special." I was dumbfounded, but we spoke briefly before I started my work.

Apart from doing a counter job, I did a behind the scenes job, too, that is, at the stairs. Once I helped inflate and distribute balloons for the store during one of their annual events. It was hot and my fingers were really sore from tying all the balloons.

The horrible internship – I was doing an internship for an MNC for 6 months, it was related to my field of study in school, but it was a horrible one, to a point I thought it was useless. The people weren't willing to teach; maybe it was because they were busy or because they knew I would leave after 6 months. And even if they taught me things, it was futile because I was not allowed to practice what I was taught such as the using of a shipping programme. And so when I raised a concern, they got taken aback. Then one day, when I was about to complete my term, I told them, "I'm wasting my time here because most of the time I'm cleaning your store rooms, why not get a maid? I'm here to learn not be your office boy to tidy your store room. And the fact that you were not willing to let me use the system shows me that you guys are not ready for improvement or to even teach" when they asked me for my feedback. The lame excuse they used for not using the programme? "We would have to pay $50 if you make a mistake and amendments are to be made." Bunch of clowns! I know that, as an intern, it's normal to buy coffee and do all the small stuff for people, that's why interns are also deemed as "expendable cheap labor" but to use us to clean your trash is nonsense. I can safely tell you that I learned way more things outside than I ever did during my internship.

It was quite an experience though; they threw everything "office" related to me, such as fixing the printing machine and coffee machines. Once my supervisor shouted at me in front of the whole office, there were about 30 people. And he said "do you want to pack up now and I can call your teacher!?" All because he said I didn't do a good job, I didn't say anything because I needed to pass the internship else I would have to waste another 6 months repeating. But it was more like he didn't look good in any way.

They had poor communication skills, couldn't take answers that were real, they were only looking for answers that would please their ego; they were looking for "Yes" men, but sadly I wasn't an idiot, and that was why I guess I was hated much because I was a thinking soldier. I know there are rooms to take instructions but they were just crappy. I guess it's working life, but just that the way the management ran the company it was like their family's business. Of which is wrong by any means; though I know there are countless types of people and the difficulties in working in an office, I still thought it was a classless move made by people who wanted to look classy but had no class or professionalism.

I wasn't the only one who had issues with the way the majority of the people worked in that floor. Many people left because the people involved were keener to play childish politics than to get work done. My then classmate's dad who was the deputy director of the company during my term as an intern left after only one year in his post, and he was an easy man to work with, he was respectable and wasn't a "politics player." I guess I wasn't the only one who had issues with those guys.

Durian shells collector - Once I was working at a durian festival and my job scope was to carry out the durians for display, and then I had to clear the durian leftovers from the bins after the customers had finished. It was a tough job because the durians were heavy, they were loaded in big baskets. Surprisingly out of all the other workers; both full timers and part timers I was the only one in which the supplier had invited repeatedly into the back of stage where durians were kept and had a feast awaiting me with durians spread across tables; with all the top quality durians such as Mao Shan Wangs (Mountain cat durians) and he said "eat as much as you like! If there's not enough I'll get my men to open more for you!" All these were not the usual practice as we were only allowed to have the leftovers at night after the event but still I ate before all. I still remembered after the event while everyone was enjoying the durians; all ate from the lowest grade of durians first but yet when He saw me he said "open up the Mao Shan Wangs! He loves it!

Ham & cheese – Growing up as a kid, I always thought it was fun and interesting to sell ham in supermarkets. But I never imagined that I'd be doing it one day myself. It was a new experience, because I learned about the different types of ham and blue cheese; I ate them on a daily basis too, my female colleague often shoved me with ham and cheese. I have to say that blue cheese isn't my cup of tea. I dealt with Salami too. A sharp blade with adjustable cuts was used in the slicing of the hams.

Arranging of milk powders – The job only commenced after operating hours of the supermarket. I went in with a couple of the company's' product visualizer, they were tasked to arrange the milk powders in a way such as it would entice parents to buy the best products from the company. I started work at 9 p.m. and ended at 2 a.m. It was then that I realized that having a kid these days would easily cost parents a fortune. A company staff told me that prices have gone up sky high, almost twice of what it was years ago. Today, a family will spend an average of $500 per week just on milk powders and diapers for an infant. That's a reason to think thrice on our spending habits.

Fast food joint call center – I used to work the night shifts right after helping out my dad during the day. I guess for me the tough part was the traveling from my dad's office to the call center. It took me about an hour; though you might think it's an hour only, the waiting time and the transferring of transport mode made me tire out faster.

When I was working there, I met a colleague - an old man, probably in his 60s who was wheelchair bound. This old man shared with me how 20 years ago he met with a freak train accident on the road involving 3 cars. He had been hit 3 times by the cars and was paralyzed waist down. He also shared how he wanted to commit suicide a couple of times as he felt useless and depressed. It was like someone stealing his valuables; his legs and its movements away from him. Imagine not being able to walk suddenly as you do daily. It's going to be extremely tough.

The money he got from the proceeds of his trial through the High Court's ruling didn't mean much. It just wasn't even close, gaining a fortune but having to live the rest of your life being wheelchair-bound just didn't seem fair on any ground.

But then he says to me, "Well, Kieroy, life has to go on, whatever happened, happened" with a smile and his eyes lighting up as he shakes my hand firmly. This man obviously knew life without limbs and turned it into life without limits. Today this man works tirelessly at the call center. There are many times in life where we feel like it's the end, time to give up. But remember this story of the old man and watch how life turns around for your good. This old man may look "weak" but I can tell you this, he is stronger than many with proper limbs.

Sneaker sales – I used to work for this established sneaker company too. The main bulk of customers were sneaker heads, many would just try and buy without asking for the price of the shoe; I guess they were really familiar with the prices. Then there were many window-shoppers, who would ask to try countless pairs of shoes without buying anything. From a sales person's point of view, though it was my job to entertain you, it has now become the reason why I do not try things unless I'm almost certain I would buy it. I'm sure people who work in the sales line would certainly appreciate it if customers are straightforward about things. If they are just window shopping they could just say so and if they are really keen, they should show it by buying it, too, maybe not immediately but they should tell you a dateline for it, so you won't waste your time hoping on hopeless hope. So many people are guilty of it, though that is another reason why money is hard- earned, but it sucks.

Today, I hardly try on clothes before I purchase them, because I know my size and I know how the different fittings of clothes would fit me – that is confidence for you. That's another reason why I'm a quick shopper and a happy one, too, simply because I don't take long to decide on things; the longer you take to decide on things, the harder it gets. But first, I'll ask about the price, and then see if I have enough and if I like it then I'll make the purchase. There is a perk in not being too huge in size or too tall, as I get to save a lot on clothes too, I could easily pick up an extra-large kid-sized basketball shorts, which is of the same design as an adult size and pay 70% of the actual price. It was a hassle for me back then, as I had to climb up the ladder and search high and low for the different models and colors of the shoes.

Door boy – Definitely not an exciting job, because all I did was to open a huge glass front door at a hotel in Sentosa for customers and greet them. I stood there the whole day; I wasn't able to do the job of a bell boy as they felt that I was too new for the job.

Traffic marshaller at a port – It was a tough Christmas, because then I really needed the money; I worked during Christmas under the sun, not even in a shopping center but an area not open to the public. There was a Roll on roll off (RORO) ship waiting to be loaded with the new cars of different makes to be shipped out of Singapore. I was given the role of a marshaller, a boring and repetitive meaningless job as I wasn't an experienced driver; they were looking for people who had a minimum one year of driving experience to drive the cars onto the vessel, and I just happened to be at the half-way point of 6 months. I just stood at one corner the entire day alone signaling the vehicles, and for someone outgoing like myself, it was even tougher as I had no one to talk to.

Part time admin – It was for a huge MNC. My working hours were initially from 8:30 a.m. to 6 p.m., but I always felt as though it started at 6 p.m. Not that I did nothing from 8:30 a.m., but because my boss, a South East Asian Regional Manager, only had time to sit down with me after office hours to discuss the things I needed to do, because he wouldn't need to attend countless meetings. Staying up till 9 p.m. was a common thing, but what made things crazier was that my boss would come in at 7 a.m. and leave at 10 p.m. almost daily. He was a good boss, and I felt appreciated and respected working for him. It's rare for someone with such a high post in the office to ask me for my opinions on getting around a certain task or how we should do things. With that, I just felt that he gives respect to me even before I proved myself. That made me go harder than I ever thought I would; going the extra mile and showing up to work earlier and leaving later. One of the things I learnt was to write down our tasks, it takes the pressure of trying to remember everything. Sometimes even with notes we forget things how much more when there's a lot of things on our mind?

Though I had limited knowledge and experience, with him opening up and giving me the room to grow as an individual taught me a lot about dealing with people. As far as I know, not too many bosses would even be keen to talk to a part-time worker let alone ask for his inputs. But he tells me he had a tough time climbing up his ladders, too; his former bosses and colleagues tried to sabotage his career by lying about him and not wanting to even help him when he needed help, therefore he understood how to treat people. In spite of all these, I wasn't too keen about gaining knowledge as I was picking his brains on life issues. To me, knowledge is easily gained, with the internet these days, I could probably get the knowledge he spent his years reading through countless textbooks and going through countless exams within a much shorter time frame.

But it was the rich life experience that he had; parenting, doing businesses with tricky unscrupulous persons and more, that I was keen on picking his brains and knowing more, that were usually the topics for our lunch. I rarely asked or talked about work, because my tasks were rather straightforward. Unlike knowledge that is gained, such can only be passed down, and it is likely that everyone would go through such things in life. As for me, I'd rather ask questions now; the mistakes people made and lessons learned through their own journey and then try to store it in my brains. So that, when the time or opportunity comes, with whatever life issues, I would know how to get around things. I know many people would like to wait until things happen before acting on it, and its fine, too, but just not for me.

I left after two months because I had to go help my relative with his business; the initial contract was 1 month, but I worked an extra month. Before I left, he asked me to stay on as there was plenty of cleaning up to do after the previous staff left abruptly, or rather she got fired for her poor performance. After I left, the job agent I had gotten the job through called me once with him calling me twice on two separate occasions to ask if I would come back to help him.

ALL ABOUT THE CARS

I do, and did everything I can and could for the car company. From washing cars to cold-calling customers to doing administrative things and attending to customers, whatever you can think of, I did. But the main thing was learning how to deal with different customers.

I believe in helping the client first before filling my pocket with profits, of course you try not to compromise on not making profits but really, I never liked the idea of a "one time deal." I prefer to have a long-lasting customer relationship, whereby, even if I do not get the deal done with you today, I believe that there will be a next time. Because it's human nature to want things that sound more attractive, but once you get the thing, you'll realize that it is nothing but junk covered in sugar. For example, I know of customers who strike a deal with another car dealer only to complain to me, "I wish I had taken your advice" or, "I wish I had gotten the car from you because now I feel it was a bad move." All I can say is, "next one will be better." Nor am I bashing other people; it's none of my business to mend any people's business but my own.

Caring for the welfare of your client is rare these days, but honestly, maybe that is the reason why some sales people can push for you to get the sales so that the main beneficiary would be their bank accounts, but then again I always wonder how is it possible for people to sleep by doing things against their conscience. I cannot do it. Maybe that's why I do not earn as much I guess, but it's better to have a good sleep over lesser profits as to no sleep over more profits, the latter will likely end up with more health issues.

But certainly, it is a challenge to balance both being assertive and not being pushy at the same time, because if you are not assertive enough, the deal is not likely to happen, but if you're too pushy, then you'll scare away the customer.

ARROGANT CUSTOMERS

It's fair to say that people who are arrogant talk a lot more than they do and are unlikely to fulfil their contract or even so they do it unhappily most of the time, such as agreeing to the full commission to be paid out to us as stipulated in the contract, but only to back out. And I find it strange how people can actually say that some kids are cocky. I mean it's natural for such parents to produce such kids because kids actually watch their actions towards other people, and just because they see their parents doing it, they grow up thinking it is right just because it came from their parents. But what goes around comes around, I guess.

Towards these things I guess it always boils down to money. Don't get me wrong, everyone would love to have the upper hand, but some do it at the expense of their reputations over a midget amount. And it is not because they can't afford it, but rather they find it hard to fulfil it because it's their money first, before their dignity, not even their principles. If money were their principle focus, I wonder how much principle they have in their lives.

I wish people would place relationship over money in every matter, but I guess it's just wishful thinking.

Dirty laundry

Growing up I've seen people use dirty tricks just to get a sale or even cheat customers. I do not do any of it, but I also know that in every industry there will some dirty laundryman and therefore as the saying goes one rotten apple spoils the whole basket. I once witnessed tampering of the car mileage. It was done by a professional, or so I would think. He did it so well; left no finger prints behind and erased markings written on the engine area that had anything to do with the mileage of the car. Still it was an eye opener, I hear stories about it, but I never imagined that I would witness it. And you might say "Why not play the police and have him nabbed?" Well, the hard truth is this – things can be technically right and justified under the law but "wrong" in terms human "rights" knowing that many are forced to do all sorts of things just to survive. Do you want to be hailed as a hero and get someone busted for his acts, knowing that he has a family to feed? I guess for me as open and "upright" as I am, there are many things I am not able to do. I know you would think about the "countless people" that I could save but I just couldn't do it then. I don't know if you could do it either. I am not a totally upright law abiding person all the time - I'm human. Though I try my best to be the best citizen out there, to be the best law keeper there are many things I believe that I'm unable to uphold all the time.

I do not say bad things about other car businesses, I only drop subtle hints if I have to because I do not want to get caught spilling the beans on other people. And I guess it's also an unwritten rule of respecting other people as well as minding your own business. But of course if I have to warn a friend I would and also would not mind making a stand if I deem that someone is trying to accuse me over something I didn't do, such as saying that I cheat people of money. I guess court is the way to go for me.

STRIKING WHILE THE IRON IS HOT

I personally like doing things spontaneously, it is the same when it comes to a deal, either buying or selling. But I guess not everyone likes the idea.

Towards selling their cars, customers often lose out because they are either always looking at the smaller picture instead of the bigger ones, or rather they aren't realistic. They'd sit all day thinking about gaining that one grand, but end up losing ten grand because the first deal came, and they weren't quick to satisfy their greed for more and many times they think that they're the only customer who has a car out there for sale. I've learned that it is better to lose a little bit, or even a little bit more than to lose much more afterwards, but still it's very difficult because it's human tendency to want to have more. I get it, but really, there are not too many people who have that much cash to let things slip by time and time again. Even the rich people seize such opportunity to either make more or cut their losses. It's the same for buyers; either they can't depart with that extra bit more of a few grand, or are likely to buy with impulse on something that is cheaper, but is of worse condition. Towards these things, generally one can tell how genuine of a customer one is. By talking about the price immediately would scare away window shoppers, but would attract the serious customers who are looking for a deal. That is the litmus test, from there then we would know whether we are wasting our time or not. Many customers talk a good game, but can't even play – they speak as though they have all the money in the world, but can't even commit or they give the power play move – make you wait by being late on purpose just to show they have control over you. It is alright to be late, but having the courtesy to let the waiting party know is only good manners.

I have to watch out for my own interests, too, I don't think any organisation would give customers a period of forever to make a decision. They know it's better to look elsewhere than to wait on one customer. For all we know; the customer might just use us as leverage against other offers. Then leave us in dust when they found a better offer. That is why I let my yes be yes, and my no be no, whenever it comes to decision making. It's easier and better for both sides. So no one wastes their precious effort and time.

Now placing myself in the shoe of a customer, I'd certainly want the best deal for myself. However, many people are sceptical whenever we give them advice, especially those with regards to the pricing of their cars; it's natural to think that "oh this guy wants to earn a fortune out of me." But come on, these days, everything is so transparent, even if I wanted to earn a few hundred off you it's already difficult enough let alone a few thousands. There are risks in every business, but with cars, you are looking at a few thousands to the tens of thousands every transaction. As I have to weigh the options even more; it's a death deal for me if I sell you a car that is in good condition today, to only break down after a couple of months because of major issues such as a spoiled gearbox and a spoiled engine. On top of it, we have bank interests and overheads to pay off.

Still, I enjoy doing business with people who are straightforward and magnanimous, this means they are happy to get a deal done even if it's more that they are losing out on, but these people are happy customers, too because they know the joy of finishing an affair quickly and mainly because they are comfortable with getting a deal done. At the end of the day, everyone wants to know and feel that they are dealing with someone who is sincere. I guess that's why the conversation, apart from the deal, makes a huge difference. People can tell if someone is genuine, they can feel it, it's unexplainable.

THE SERIOUS ONES COME RELAXED

There are all sorts of buyers, the big talkers who only talk and the one who comes in with shorts. I have dealt with customers who are covered in branded goods from head to toe, only to be disappointed greatly by their poor demeanour; they talk a good game and make you wait as though they are the only people in the world but rarely buy anything. They enjoy showing "power" by striking a pose – hands folded else it's on their hips. Than we have the other extreme, customers walking in with shorts and are direct and straight to the point. They tell you their budget and are quick to get a deal done. They are nice people who understand that both our time and theirs are of equal value; we all go through that one hour doing the same thing. May not be in terms of salary but they understand how it's like to be treated fairly and to treat others the same. The best part? They know that it's their money that makes the world's economy going – it may be just a drop of water in the ocean but certainly it makes a whole lot of difference. It also tells me that these people are not too hard up on money—it's one thing to have money and be stingy and another to have less money and still be generous.

TRUST AND RELATIONSHIPS COME AND GO LIKE CARS

Sadly, this is the truth for many industries. First they learn, then they create their own company. It is hard for me to respect someone who takes something from you and then jumps ship, to me that is downright shallow. It isn't wrong for someone to want to have their own business. However, being honest about it will make people give you their blessings freely. But the way they get out of things, by not giving the truth makes one look weak and shallow. Age does not define one's character but the excuses drown your character.

On the other hand, sometimes the hardest businesses to do are with friends'. Because we are close it makes it hard to tell the other party their wrongs or even talk commission. Towards these things, there are times where friends play us out, I'm not talking coincidence, I'm talking on purpose (but then again which robber leaves his fingerprints behind?) but it's rather obvious that people act as though they are willing to deal with you, give you the green light and when it's time to sign the deal, they quit. Citing all sorts of reasons, to me it's simple, I won't lose sleep over it, but surely your character is as cheap as the value of the product.

Everywhere an experience

As a result of these jobs, I had the chance to go to places that are at times not opened to customers or public. It's an eye opener, because I know I'll likely never enter a warehouse, a storage area and even a room where people keep coffins. Throughout all these, the most valuable skill I gained was the Personal Relationship skill – the skill to talk to people. I also learned how to differentiate people and their characters. It makes things easier because now I know if I should leave early or stick with them

During my national service; my duty, a fellow comrade in arms passed on and I had the opportunity to take part in a military funeral to be a flag bearer. It's one thing to be part of a procession but another to take part in a military's. It's rare even for Singapore, and I had the chance. I would think it's a once in a life time experience. Because it wasn't common, many people whipped out their phones to record down the process. And there was a place at the columbarium whereby the coffin was kept before it was pushed out to show family and friends for the last time, and I happened to be in a room with the coffin. It was surreal and a little scary. But still it was an eye opening experience.

On another occasion, I was selected to be an ambassador for SAF50. This event was to commemorate the 50th year of the introduction of National Service. Singapore as a nation has come a very long way. Initially, I thought I would be just an ambassador to the public, little did I know I was actually an ambassador to the Minister of Defense, Minister of State for Defense and their entourage. I only had a day to prepare for it as I got the news only the day before. It's so amazing how I got picked for an event that occurs only once in fifty years let alone an ambassador to the top officials. It's also my first time being in front of a dozen cameras at the same time.

Life becomes more meaningful if we go through certain things because through it, we'll understand that there are many things we've yet to learn, how to appreciate things and when to ignore people. It puts a lot of things into better perspective, and that is why I write.

The next section will look at things inclined towards life, it's a continuation about work, but more towards what I see and feel about life in relation to work. Let's face it, life is bigger than work. Even though we may spend more than half of our entire life at work, but without life, there is no work, and so I feel the importance to write a little about life considering the fact that I have spent a large chunk of this book writing about work and the importance of it. It is not facts and figures that I'm into or selling because facts change while the truths remain. As far as writing a book based on knowledge, it isn't my cup of tea, because I have no PhDs and years of countless knowledge about science or the economy, but rather what I have and know, I proudly give it to you in hope that it could either widen your perspective or hopefully you would understand where I'm coming from.

I hope you're enjoying this book so far, even if you are offended I hope it doesn't sway you from reading on and that it would give you a new perspective on work. Especially coming from someone who feels like he is mentally older but stuck in time, or rather a soul waiting to get moving towards another chapter of life. Writing this book today, I am 22 years of age, and am currently awaiting to complete my National Service, and then I'll see where life will take me, time will never stop moving and that is why I am also in a fight against time to get things done considering what little time I have.

After going through different things in life, the various experiences and gaining knowledge and wisdom, I realize that at the end of the day, we play a huge role in our lives. Way larger than what we think we know. This book relies solely on my opinions, thoughts and experiences or rather an Ideology that I'd like to share with you.

"It's not about the money, but the experience"

I've always heard a lot of parents telling their kids the above, and I think it's only partly true. Imagine working without pay, you could do it probably for a few days and that's all, because we all need money to survive: money for food, money for health, money for transport and I'm not even talking about extravagant spending on branded items that die with the trend. Alright I know you might think "oh you're dumb, it's only a figure of speech." Hear me out, I know where you're coming from, so why don't you try working for free for the next few hours, and see if we come to the same conclusion.

Though gaining experience is important, I believe the remuneration plays a large factor in the decision as well, of course there has to be a time whereby you'll say "it's alright not to get that larger pay check because I have enough or I prefer staying home than to relocate elsewhere alone." After all these things I have gone through, I know for sure hunger can come whether you are well paid or not; it's a personal thing, but if you say that your hunger to work and strive harder is solely based on the remuneration then I feel sorry for you. But certainly there's added pressure to perform better when you get a higher pay, but still that shouldn't be the main reason; it could be an added factor, but certainly not the main factor, at least for me that's how I think.

Through all these, I've learned to communicate better with people, get some much needed PR (Personal Relationship) skills that are real, unlike those that are fixed within a classroom setting whereby you're comfortable because everyone's your friend. And it helped me get more confident when approaching and talking to people, strangers especially. Something that I have grasped throughout all this is experience and a little bit of "visualising" what will happen next, to go one step ahead of others before the move even happens. I hope to learn much more in this area than any other area, because it is something that cannot be taught, but rather gained, or passed down.

Now, as a customer, after going through these experiences, I've learned to follow the guidelines given by the enforcer; because I have been in their place and know the difficulties they face, and it isn't just about telling a single customer the same thing repeatedly which is annoying enough but rather countless other customers who only think for themselves. For example not to go past the barricades just so I can take an up-close picture of a display or returning an item back to its original place that I've decided not to purchase. It sounds simple and rather a question of personal conduct. But ask yourself how many times have you gone against the instructions of the person working?

PLAY NICE AND OTHERS WILL TOO

People always think that it is the cashier or waiter's duty to be nice, to be polite and smiling all the time, and that it is on them to give the customer a good service, which is true, but we all know that there are countless types of servers with different attitudes, some are rude, some work unhappily and they show it on their sleeves and more. But what I'd like to highlight here is that you as a customer can actually dictate the type of service you get. Yes, granted that it is not possible all the time with people but it's still on you more often than you think, hear me out before you jump the gun to "it's their job! I'm paying indirectly to their salary by patronising their food joint!" If you treat the server with respect, this means you greet them, joke with them, and give them a compliment before they even get your order, there is a higher tendency that your food would have more stuffs added, and no I'm not talking about the "extra stuffs" you get when you offend the waiter or waitress, or you are more likely to have someone treating you better. Such as attending to you promptly even if the restaurant is full or maybe even get you a dessert that is on the house, you get my point? These people are human, too, it's just that they do a different day job from you, so treat them the way you'd like to be treated if you were in their place, too.

When it comes to taking orders, imagine this: a family of five being seated and a waiter comes over to take the family's orders. The waiter first starts with the dad, and before the dad finishes his order, the mom interrupts with another other, and then the kids follow their parents lead. How then do you expect the waiter not to make mistakes? I really do not and cannot understand the difficulty of waiting for the waiter to finish writing down the current order and then you making your order. And I thought this was a combination of patience, manners, and common sense, but I guess it's hard to juggle knowing when to use any one of these three at one time.

Once I was at a Subway, and I noticed that the customer in front of me was really rude. When he was told by the server that it would cost him more to have more meat added to his sandwich, he hurled vulgarities at the guy and said "I'm filthy rich you think I can't afford it? Hurry up!" The server was never rude to begin with. Seeing these from the back, I couldn't help but get involved, so I "spoke" to a friend beside me and said, "Well, bro, money can buy you a lot of things, but I guess manners and respect is not something that can be bought." As I was saying these things I was looking towards him, and I was hoping he'd start something with me so I could continue to take pleasure in bruising his ego. It was a sad plight for him; he was much taller, about one and a half head and way bigger, he probably weighed 20 kg more than me. But he couldn't even look me in the eye; he left immediately after paying for his meal. At the end of my meal, I went back to look for the "abused" employee and told him "don't worry, you're doing a great job, people come and go, but keep your joy"

Maybe the reason why those who can be patient and nicer most of the time to those working in the customer service line is probably because of whatever they've gone through, and I know it is tough. I hope to make the life of such people easier, because it really isn't easy to be on the receiving end all the time. And though there are positive feedbacks, the negative ones dwarf them and with just one negative feedback, someone could lose their job in spite of all the ten good ones.

"CUSTOMERS ARE ALWAYS RIGHT"

The only people who would say such a thing are the ones who either have never worked in the service industry or are a difficult customer themselves. As much as you'd like to think that I'm wrong, I'll give you a simple reason why I'm right, simply because we're all humans and humans are never right all the time. Regardless of how good one is or one may think they are, it's never possible to have never had a brush off with a customer. I'm not talking about handling things with professionalism, yes there are ways to handle difficult people, but I'm talking about people who say that as professionals we ought to have a perfect record. Sometimes, even if you do not look for trouble, trouble will look for you, just because it's an ugly thing. And you certainly would not be saying that customers are always right if they'd just give you a punch for no reason, even a punch as a result of a dispute is also wrong.

HAVE YOU EVER DESPISED THEM?

Growing up in a developed country, we've all come across foreign workers, and we often think that just because they do not work in offices or earn a five figure income that we are superior to them. I'm talking about the Bangladesh and Indian workers who work their lives in the hard labor construction industry. These poor men, work 7 days a week; all because they need the money to survive, or to send money home for their loved ones. It's already hard enough to work 7 days a week and still they are separated from their loved ones thousands of miles away. On top of it, they do not have the luxury to fly home as and when they like because not only do they lack the money, but also it's likely for them to be fired as they're counted on to work long hours.

Now if you think you have a tough job, look at how these men earn their bread and butter., which is considered low, and then also look at their sleeping conditions; whereby it's normal to sleep only 6 hours per night and squeeze in a small room that has some 6 to 10 other men in it. Whether the weather is good or bad; rain or shine, they still work their butts off. Be it in their sweat or when they're drenched in the rain.

While working as a Maintenance Representative I had a chance to work with countless foreign workers and got to see first-hand how they worked round the clock under different weather conditions just to get things done. I'm not saying that everyone has to go through what they go through, I believe we all have different lives, but it'll be good to at least know how tough times could shape one's character to be humble and also appreciative of things. I think if more people were to be exposed to these things, then the selfishness and insecurity of each individual would certainly be in check. These men, despite having little to nothing, always seem joyful, all because they share the burdens of every other counterpart working beside them and know that simplicity beings happiness.

MISTAKES ARE TO BE MADE

Certainly not on purpose though, very often people cannot improve because they do not make mistakes or even enough and therefore do not know what went wrong or how to improve on things. So often people shy away from doing things that they know would get them ahead in life or are afraid to be criticised for making mistakes, but that is the only way to grow. So often we hear things like "I'm afraid to make mistakes" In life as far as making mistakes goes, the more cautious you are, it is more likely that you will make more mistakes; because you've unknowingly become mistake-conscious, and this becomes your natural state. But, of course, the point is not to do it on purpose, but rather take it as a lesson should it happen. If you never make a mistake, you'll have nothing to take away.

It is just like tree pruning; and it might hurt at the start. Sometimes tree pruning comes as a result of selective removing of parts of a plant for the main purpose of improving and maintaining health. Making mistakes lets you know that not only are you human but also shows that there's room for improvement – the biggest room in the world. So your mistakes should not hinder you.

However, when it comes to taking criticism, no one really likes it; there are two parts to it, being open and knowing when to close the door. Firstly determine whether it is constructive criticism that is good for you then knowing how to work on things, to this open your door. But close your doors on things said by someone out of jealousy just so they can knock you off. I read this short story about making mistakes at work, I'm very sure it'll help change your perspective.

"Dan a lab technician, had forgotten to check some sort of mechanism on a piece of equipment he used, it malfunctioned and broke the equipment which ended up having a repair bill of $250,000. The next day Dan's boss called him in to talk about it, and he was sure he was going to be fired. His boss asked him why he didn't do a proper check, made sure he understood what had happened and sent him back to work. Dan asked him "am I not getting fired?" His boss replied "No way, I just spent $250,000 teaching you a lesson you'll never forget, why would I fire you now?"

Certainly we would fire the worker since it's a lot of money that he blew up, but you know this story shows us that we should not make professional decisions based on our emotions. Always know what your goal is when dealing with someone and the exact problem you are trying to solve. Everyone makes mistakes, yelling at people makes them resent you and become defensive. Whereas, being calm and understanding will make people look up to you.

Only people who don't work make no mistakes, and only people who work to improve make mistakes. After all, life is a seed and some mistakes are fertilizer for growths.

THE CHALLENGE TO BALANCE

We all wish to work with our friends but it's not possible, mainly because we all have different paths to walk in life, but even in a fairy-tale arrangement whereby all the good buddies could come and work together it's still not likely to work well.

Firstly, we all react differently to adversities, and because of our different personalities it's hard enough to get everyone on the same page, you're not talking about coming out to have a party or even coffee, but work, whereby there are deadlines to meet and things to be done. And sometimes the obstacles are not entirely work-related but relationship-related, which will put one in a dilemma; should I tell him to get cracking? Or should I just wait since he's my friend as I do not want to offend him or put a strain on our friendship.

It's a thin line, and sometimes people take things differently; you know it's not possible to have all the time in the world to stop, think, analyze and rethink about what he or she said and tell yourself, "maybe he didn't mean what he said, or maybe he said things out of anger." For me sometimes I find it hard, too. As someone who can't wait to finish things as soon as possible, I do admit that I'll drag along everyone into the cockpit and race to the finishing line, and I know not everyone is cool with it, but that's how I work. I can't sit around and wait for things to happen. That's why for me, if I had a choice I'd like to have teammates who are generally ready to go to "war" every time, but also it'll be great if I have someone to tell me to slow down once in a while. You know, it's like telling me where I might step on a landmine because I'm too aggressive. I do not mind playing commando all the time, but there are times whereby I need to just let others take over. Having people with different skill sets to accommodate me or me accommodating them is great.

As far as I could remember during all my presentations, I was in charge of presenting because I had a better presenting skill whereas, because of my flaw in doing power point slides, it would be done by others, however, I do take the lead often when it comes to researching and directing the direction of the group.

Still, I know when I should lead or go with the flow like water, because I know that there are times I have to just zip up and listen to others, for they know better. I may not be the best person to work with because I take work very seriously; I know that I may come off as a threat to others as well even the older colleagues but the only reason I think I can be a threat to them is because they are lazy. I hate working with people who lack work ethic, it sucks, and it's hard for me to want to get to know you better or even have a drink with you. Everyone has issues outside of work: family, financial, health, and more, but it shouldn't be an excuse to slack off every single day. We all have days where we are not at our best, that's fine because we're mere humans. But to have that mind-set and to do things subpar on a regular basis, it means you just downright suck. The thing is this – if we struggle to work together when we face each other hours a day, I think it is very unlikely we will be buddies outside of the office. That is why I say that it is a challenge to balance a good relationship in and out of the office.

What I think makes one respected

Certainly work ethic. Everything starts with work ethic and, of course, attitude. But the willingness to do things that people aren't willing to do; to go the extra mile certainly would make me want to respect someone, even if I could not stand his behavior or character. It's simple and straight-forward.

But with that said, of course knowing what role to play, leaving when you have to and what shoes to fill, I guess it isn't always about "I'm more senior and therefore I won't do it." But rather sacrifice to just get things done, to make things easier for everyone else, and it is a hard thing to do for people who have their pride glued to their position and "me-first" mind-set. With leaving when I have to or rather as I would call it good-quitting. Sometimes we just have to keep our dignity and just walk away because there are better things out there, people would want us, people who need us and people who respect us.

To me I think it'd be great if people could actually do what it takes to get things done instead of kicking a fuss. I know it's very hard to do, I struggle with it at times, too, because I'm human and I get tired and, more importantly, I am narcissistic to a certain extent and want things done my way. With that said, I know that I do not cross people's comfort boundaries, or rather that's what I think, and it may not be true, but, for sure, I know that I just happen to extend the boundaries when it comes to getting things done, such as pushing people. And that is probably why I think it isn't that easy or fun to work with me, 'cause I'll tell you straight in your face what you need to do.

With these said, I have to admit that I do not always get along well with my peers but bosses just love the job done by me; it's because I get things done, I guess, and that is what they are most concerned with. Still, I know it is very important to get along well with peers or colleagues at work because they could plot a plan to destroy me.

WHAT ARE YOU DOING?

In this modernized era of a fast-paced, stressful and deteriorating life, we often miss out on the good part simply because it is a whole lot easier, more attractive, and more tempting to give in to the negative and down side of life, and before long we would've missed the bigger and more important picture. This quote *"The trick to forgetting the big picture is to look at everything close up."* by Chuck Palahniuk' explains the above. Despite knowing these, we often find ourselves trying to do the impossible - to go back and try to redo everything, when in the midst of going through that tough time we could have (almost as easily) changed our perspective.

This section is simple, upfront and as-is, five different areas in which, if we change our negative perspective, would certainly improve our lives.

Seeing – When it comes to seeing, do you see only the downside? Do you have myopia? Human Myopia to be exact. So what is human myopia? It is a condition whereby the person sees only the current situation that is usually bad and chooses to ignore the further and brighter situation afar. This causes relationships to break down faster than either expected or last shorter than preferred. Things would have or could have been much better if one would have looked at things that have already been done (good and happy memories) and/or to the possibility of a higher probability that better things are coming your way. Can you recall the pointer envision the final product earlier? Seeing is one of the most effective ways that affects and impacts our lives, but it will only do you good if you would see things the right way, if you look the right way, you can see that the whole world is a garden.

What if I don't see but hear things only? Then hearing is for you.

Hearing - Have you ever been in conversations whereby you hear either all the bad stuff or either all the good stuff (rarely) or both? Which was better? You'd wish for a third choice that has both so you could pick and choose whatever you want to hear, right? However, we all know that the chance of hearing all the good stuff comes as rarely as a Lamborghini Veneno. But don't ever walk away from any of these conversations empty handed. Know what to do, just like how you'd pick the good apples out of a box of rotten apples, do the same thing. Have you heard of the phrase,

"Praise does wonders for our sense of hearing?" Well, what if they were sarcastic, or all bad stuff? Unlike fake fruits that cannot be eaten, words are seeds and in words there are no real or fake seeds rather just a matter of quality regardless of whom it came from. And if it's good take them, for hearing good things refreshes one's soul and body. And if they are of bad quality throw them away like how you'd dispose your used tissue!

And what about my feelings? What if I get affected by the things I see or hear?

Feelings - As creatures with feelings, it is not always easy to tackle or handle one's feelings, but it is not impossible. The best way to deal with feelings is to shake them off like dust on your shoes before they take root. However, things get more complicated when it comes to those close to us or near our hearts. Your loved ones, or colleagues do this or that and your feelings get smashed to the ground like a broken glass. But there's something I've learned, be it a good or bad feeling we've to deal with it. It's always easier to move across a drain than a running stream of river water, though it might take more effort and time, we've got to deal with it. There's always a season for mourning but there's something better called - A life of joy. In this case it's more than having the right perspective, but also knowing the time limit for mourning. You can either choose to be known as the person who gets knocked-out or the person who gets knocked down but never out! I think the latter sounds more sexy and attractive! One piece of advice - if you want someone to open up about their feelings to you, start off by having the same base for connection, but even if you do not have the same base, be genuine, trust will develop over time and with trust things are more likely to work out. The world is tragedy for those who feel, and a platform for comedy for those who think.

And what if those thoughts are already in? Or I can't stop thinking about them?

Thinking - When it comes to our thoughts, sometimes knowing less is knowing more! All through the day, if you are going to let thoughts get to your head, it'd better be good and positive thoughts as much as you can, considering the fact that negative news are more popular, and attractive and outnumber the positive ones. Listen to good recordings on life, read a positive article, or the Bible, or communicate with someone who's positively charged like Energizer! Leave the presence of someone negative who chants out negative reports faster than a shooting machine gun! Before you know it, you'll be a body full of negativity caused by negative bullets! The rationale behind this is simple: be careful of your thoughts; they may become words at any moment. Just like how superstar players hate to play the role of a bench-warmer, and would ask for a trade without hesitating— start by substituting your bench warmers(negative thoughts) with positive ones(superstar players), before long you would see a whole new world!

Now, if you are not cautious with what you see, hear, feel, or think you probably might want to consider speaking first.

Speaking –

To speak and to speak well are two things. A fool may talk but a wise man speaks. Everyone can talk, but not all can speak. The main difference is the thing that comes out from one's big mouth. Not everyone has the gift of gab; some have the gift of talking one's ear off. But having gifts, and not knowing how to fully utilize them is as good as saying, I'm alive but I live in a coffin. The thing about speaking is that it is recycled in to you, because you are the first to say it and hear it. So if you had a choice, would you rather have good things going back and through you or bad, destructive things? Knowing the power and importance of your words, would not only allow you to decide over your future, but also bring blessings over those near and around you.

Want to know the power of positive speaking? This is what the African tribe does: when someone does something hurtful and wrong, they take the person to the center of town, and the entire tribe comes and surrounds him. For two days they'll tell the man every good thing he has ever done. There you go, it's amazing how at times we think that we who live in the world of globalization and have all the answers through the internet often miss out on the real deal – how the world without globalization has a better way to get around life than the world of the internet. What paradox, but such truth; the more connected we get, the more isolated we feel.

SOLVING THE FEAR MYSTERIES

Fear of being alone; eating alone

So many kids have this fear when they first start work, to a point where they'd rather skip their meals just because they are afraid of eating alone. Once you've grown you kind of understand that it is normal, and better to fill your stomach than to go hungry. It's hard at first, but sometimes it's the best thing within your day of work. Because every single moment of your customer service line, you are practically surrounded by people, everywhere you go you see people to the point where you'll get sick of them. But it is only during these alone times during breaks that you have your own me-time. And you'll learn to appreciate it eventually. Personally, I dislike going to crowded places, I prefer places that are less crowded and quiet, it's like an opportunity to gain back your own conscience, rest, and get yourself ready again. And I certainly do not have Ochlophobia – the fear of crowds

FEAR OF SPECIFIC PHOBIA; BOSSOPHOBIA

When talking to someone of a greater stature; someone who is more senior in terms of rank or post, I generally still see them as human; so I don't get all nervous and make myself look weak. Of course, you'll think it's a straightforward stupid thing to even think or say, but ask yourself this, "How many times have I gone speechless when talking to someone powerful?" Of course I'm not saying that it doesn't happen to me, but I guess it's relatively few. If I have choices between standing up to speak and maybe embarrassing myself over a "stupid" question and to stay quiet and not learn anything, I'll take the former every single time. Because I get to clarify my doubts, and it's a better feeling than being doubtful all the time. Certainly your manners, and right attitude, and tone have to be there; it's a must because more than anything it's a reflection of yourself, how you carry yourself. Do you carry yourself confidently? Sometimes, I know I do get into the other party's head instead of them getting into mine. I'll show up and speak with more confidence than they will ever expect from someone "small." But in actuality, the only explanation I can think of when doing such a thing (and also because I do not know how to put it down in words) is that generally at the back of my head I'll think, *I don't care who you are or where you're from, I'll just do or say whatever I need or have to.* That is the essence for me, I guess, but you can be sure I don't tell them that, of course! I just allow myself to have that idea so I won't freak out.

WORKING FIELD

When it comes to work, I think it's a lot like soccer; on the soccer field we have things that are going on that we are oblivious to, or rather it is because we are more focused on the ball than the players away from the ball. Sometimes things are obvious, sometimes they aren't. For example, office politics; it may not seem obvious to you at first, but once you notice certain people starting to treat you differently, such as moving away from you when you show up, then you know it's an issue, and obvious. Towards choosing sides and office politics—I would think that it is a childish game played by full-grown adults; maybe they didn't have a childhood? I don't know, but only immature and weak people play politics to climb the ranks. To me, it's a very shallow move, it's simple, because if you're meant to get the promotion, you'll get it, else there's no point in starting a political warfare. Imagine if you got the promotion by displacing a colleague through spreading lies about him or her, then your next biggest worry is to watch your back all the time, and for sure it isn't an easy job. You'll be stressed out and you're more likely to turn and look over your shoulder all the time, and if you're not careful, you'll run into a wall without knowing it because your main concern is that someone would backstab you, and then you'll cause your own death.

But, of course, we all know that it is impossible to not have such a situation all the time, and it is likely that wherever you work, there'll be politics to play, and if you're not careful you'll be dead. (And I thought humans were beautiful creatures until you see them at work). Towards these things, I know it'll get one very frustrated and angry, then you'll question why he or she likes to get under your skin or inside your head just for fun. But it's actually really simple to get around things. Generally, I'll ignore them if I feel like they are disrespectful or trying to provoke me, and also because I know I'm way better than their childish play. I mean, if I wanted to play with kids I'd look for a cute, adorable, and lovable one, not one that is full grown, ugly, and immature. The thing about ignoring people's irritating acts is that it acts as a shield and a time bomb for you. Not only do you protect yourself, but on the offensive end, the other party is likely to self-destruct because it'll be extremely frustrating for them because they've spent great efforts yet it's futile. Even dogs bark for no reasons. Research shows that kids would rather be yelled at than be ignored; it'll probably hurt more for an adult with a proper state of mind. It is better not to waste your energy and mood on someone, whose main motive is to annoy you. To get further we need to ignore these idiots; it's your life you're talking about, and you've only got one life so don't waste it on people who enjoy wasting their life away.

You want to feel even better about yourself? Or rather feel good about ignoring idiots? Science is now showing that shunning or ignoring rather than arguing is a more effective and powerful weapon against such people. On top of that, acknowledging stupidity makes one stupid and ineffective apart from ruining your day. If that isn't enough, the study in the Journal of Social and Personal Relationships also concluded that ignoring others during adverse social interactions helps one conserve mental resources. Though it is also Science that claims that people who use sarcasm are smarter, I think you'll be the smartest if you understood it and ignored it.

To a certain extent, playing mind games or having someone play mind games with you is inevitable. I have to admit that I get a kick out of playing it sometimes; it makes me feel good and human, it makes me know that I am alive and my mental focus is there; it's strong enough. However, there are times when we cannot walk away, for example, being stuck in the same group for a project; then you might probably want to talk about other things not related to work first, because it would enhance communications between parties and help people coordinate group activities better.

Work isn't tough. Maybe it is, but when you think about the politics and how people treat you, then you'll realize that it's actually not that tough; the toughest part would be working with difficult people who give all sorts of attitude and tantrums; it's like working with monkeys in human forms. It also doesn't help that sometimes people behave differently around others, yes we all have times where we are different in different situations around different people, but I refer to hypocrites here. They smile at you or say good things to you just so you could help, but they backstab you behind your back. This I cannot tolerate, it just shows me how weak they are as persons who have no character or whatsoever. Nothing that makes me want to get to know you better. Sometimes, all it takes is one guy to down the whole team.

Out in the working field, there is no such thing as fair play or equal ground. Unlike how we all start at the same age when we start play school, and graduate from school around the same age with some exceptions of a few years, no one really cares about how old you are. They just give it to you straight and expect you to deal with it. Just because you qualify for the job or fit the bill's description they think you know every single thing. And that's what you call crazy people.

When it comes to work, no one can work alone; you may think a CEO is that great, which is true. But without those people supporting him from below, completing his work orders and preparing things for him, he wouldn't be up there. For in a multitude of people is the glory of a king, but without people a prince is ruined. There is great emphasis on learning and being open with each other, that is the way towards healthy growth. Not one whereby someone teaches you half of what he knows in fear that you would one day overtake him. That I think is insecurity on his part.

Even the CEO needs constant encouragement because he's human too. I think it is very important to have friends at work, it's important to have at least a friend who is there for you when you need them at work. You don't need 10 colleagues to trust and believe you, though it's great if you have them but in reality both you and I know it's not about the numbers but quality. At times the more people you think are for you are actually the ones plotting secretly against you. Above all these things, for me I guess it is really important to have someone look out for me too, I have my blind spots as well, and it is impressible to look at every corner all the time, so a friend is what I look out for apart from completing my task.

ARE YOU SATISFIED?

It's so easy to talk about satisfaction level; I hear it all the time, just in a negative way. I often hear "I'm not happy" or "I'm not satisfied" and then with the common replies "Its life" or "don't worry you'll get used to it." I wish people would understand that life is just a blink of an eye. Why not leave if you aren't happy? Then of course people will have a comeback and say "I cannot walk away because I'm too old and I need the money, it's hard to find a job outside."

That's why it's so important to at least know a little of what you like to do and do it for life, it's impossible to know everything, and at times you just cannot do what you like either because there isn't a chance or you cannot survive on doing it because the pay is too low.

Towards getting more satisfaction, I think it's like you get what you give; the more effort you put in the more satisfaction you get. But of course it all starts with doing something you like, it's like the closer something is to you the more it'll make sense that effort and satisfaction goes hand in hand. That's why I do things that are not related to money in hope that it brings me both joy and wealth; that means my decisions are not swayed by money to a huge extent, because regardless of whatever the outcome, I still need money to survive and that is why there must be a minimal baseline to it.

TOLERANT LEVEL

This is something that I think is very attractive. To some it's natural to have a high tolerant level towards people and their mistakes at work to some it is grown. I guess it's something that I'm trying to improve on. But as far as I know it is not something easy to gain, especially if you're impatient towards things like myself. I know that it is important because it doesn't cause you to lose your joy easily and still allows you to function at a high level at work, I think a good way is to not take things too personally.

This is how I work

I may not be a boss or yet, I do not know if I will be a boss but so far I live by this motto whenever I work "Think like a boss and work like an ant." It's just amazing how ants work; they work together, they have great working endurance and they are strong.

Work as though the company is yours, (alright I know it sounds crazy) then how about work as though you can make a huge difference? I know many people just work simply for the pay check, month after month and then they realize that after a few months they feel like job hopping, and I'll tell you why you have such an idea. Because you never possess your job with passion and you do things aimlessly just to kill time all the way until pay day and then the cycle repeats. Don't treat your job like a toy, on a macro level you may think "oh well it doesn't matter what I say or do, I'm just a small fry." But then something will happen; as a result of such a mind-set, you do not take things seriously and then you become callous with your attitude and your words. And then one day, just because of your single action or word, the company gets itself into big trouble, such as a lawsuit or even worse it closes down. Now the main thing here is this, though you might be re-employed almost instantly the following day by another company, your former company is in a dire state and you know why it doesn't mean a thing to you? Because you were not the person laying the bricks to build up the company and therefore you will never know the anguish and depression of the boss.

I think more people will be happier if they had such a motto, and they could be happy even though they do not get such a great pay, yes being well paid is important but if you are solely after money then what difference does it make you from every other employee? I think it is better to be contented with what you do or are doing before the pay comes, because once you get the increase, you won't be happy. I am for pay raise and being well paid because I believe in an abundant life, a life where you have much more than enough for yourself but also enough to bless others, after all happiness starts by giving.

Earlier I gave Oxford's definition of work. But my definition of work is "an ongoing movement that is either useful to you or others. It should be towards a goal, and the goal would be fruition that leads to satisfaction and unspeakable joy." It could be a hobby or interest or something that you've always wanted to do. Take time out to work on it. Don't let your fear and doubts turn your dreams into heartbreak

I hope that one day; it'll come to a point whereby I no longer have to introduce myself when I step into a room because I'm known for my work ethic. Though it has happened before as you've read about it above during my working experiences, but I hope it carries on throughout my entire life.

GRADUATE FROM THE SCHOOL OF HARD KNOCKS FIRST

Every other person regardless of age would love to be their own boss, simply just so they can call the shots. But that's short sightedness for you. We all crave power but not everyone can handle it. Being a boss sounds fun and powerful, but in actual fact, it is stressful and the amount of uncertainty and level of commitments are sky high, so many people think that being a boss is easy and fun. True that being a boss allows you to have the final say, but the stress of having to look beyond now and prepare for the future is a heavy burden, sometimes we think "it's a good trade-off for a high pay." But if you ask them, they will actually tell you "no, it isn't fun and being a worker is less pressurising, at the end of the day you still get paid, whereas I have to source for your next pay."

It's an eye opener when you first become your own boss; there are many things you need to know, above all it is the human aspect that I deem the most important. Though you may employ people to work for you and delegate jobs to them, it's still vital to know how to run the show alone, at least most of it, and, of course, with all of the work essentials as mentioned above. But still many youngsters lack not only experience but skills and knowledge as well. The strongest point that fails them is that, though they may not have to deal with clients directly, they neither know how to handle rejections and failures from the start. And that is when the snowball starts to roll. If one cannot handle rejections and failures, what makes you think they know how to motivate and keep their employees going after they have failed? The word resilient is a verb, an action word. It takes actions to make it work, and knowing that such is the reality of successful business – motivated and happy workers. Are you ready? Can you motivate others around you? Are you even self-motivated and resilient? There are rooms and different periods in life where you may feel like you might want to take the leap of faith – to be your own boss. Maybe you've reached a point whereby you feel as though you have the experience and funds. The only thing I know that can keep things going is to lead by example. Not by mere talking for talk is free. Bosses should always lead by example, they should be the reflection that they want to see in their people. This means that they should be or strive to be the figure that they'd like to attract around themselves.

A SHIP HAS MANY CADETS

Do you think it is possible to keep an eye on everyone? Or even make all the decisions?

I think a successful company is one that does not have a structure that is too stringent and too structured. Though it is a must, allowing others to take control; to make minor decisions on their own and only to consult you the boss with regards to greater decisions, this way not only does it lighten your load but it promotes a workforce of thinking workers. I am against micromanagement but for macro management because it builds trust and encourages workers to work harder because they feel free, this in turn would bring growth for the company.

HAPPY WORKERS, HAPPIER BOSS

I love this quote "if you take care of your people, your people will take care of your customers and your business will grow by itself." So many bosses only desire for an extra zero for their bank account at the end of the year but never for once stopped to look and wonder if their workers are happy. A good boss is patient and generous. A good boss shows up and works harder than employees. A great boss is one who does not sit entirely in his large office and make policy-changes or pass down rules just so it makes his job easier; but rather he goes down to the floor, the place where the dirty jobs are done, the place where people do not earn even close to what he earns and from there makes his decisions, because only then will he know how will certain changes affect people. Of course it's impossible to do it all the time; in fact it is never possible to please everyone but the main thing is to ensure that your changes are done with the benefit of people, especially of those on the receiving end.

To add on, people want to feel appreciated and recognised, no one likes to go unnoticed after working their butts off. If they know they are appreciated they would certainly work even harder.

A TIME AND SEASON FOR EVERYTHING

At the end of the day I have to admit that I do admire how Japanese people work, but not totally because of Karo-shi which means death from too much work. I do respect them for their drive, sacrifice, and loyalty but also I think it is a thin line between over working and working smart. Therefore it would be good to have a balance between the Japanese and French; that encourage shorter but more productive hours. Many researchers are also citing that working more than 40 hours a work is useless and makes you exhausted. I do not think that the main reason behind it is financial even though France has a strong economy, but then the main point I think that makes the French people productive is because they are happy. Again, happy workers equal to more production and more production equals to happier bosses.

WORK; A LIFE

In closing, with all the importance about work, life comes first and will always be more important than work. For I know that there is nothing better for people than to be happy and to do good while they live. I would also like to tell people: Do not work with a chip on your shoulders to prove others wrong; what if the person you are trying to prove wrong dies? Are you going to stop? So many people die to themselves and live just to please others, it's sad. And I do things to get them done not to please anyone. Work like you are a proven substance. This is definitely a higher level and brings out better work ethic and also it differentiates you from your peers; your boss will value you more too, trust me. It's funny how work brings us so much pressure, stress, and nights without sleep, yet in returns gives us joy, pleasure, and blessings that come only from work.

But when there is no work, then we should do life; make life, or rather more life, happen. I'm constantly working to learn to put work aside and do life, because it seems like I always have work stored at the back of my mind, and I know it is not healthy. Physically, I may look distracted with thoughts of working, but on a more important note, I'm not able to enjoy the company of those around me. Go out with your loved ones, meet up with your friends, discuss things pertaining to life; it beats wasting time and money on valuables that do not enrich you but makes you poorer.

I thank God for allowing me to go through these things, for giving me insights and wisdom but above all helping me grow as an individual. At the end of the day I still am a work in progress; working and learning never stops. As much as I know, the number one thing that keeps me going and sane is spending time with God, reading the Bible and talking to the right people that believe in the same thing and work towards it.